TRACKS OF LONDON'S TRAMS

1949-1952

Robert J Harley

Heathfield Publishing

Cover Beneath the chimneys of Woolwich Power Station, car 2053, having stowed its trolley pole, is about to proceed taking power from the conduit. Note the architecture of the pub and adjacent shops, which dated to the late Victorian era. Who now remembers OAKEY'S EMERY CLOTH or WISK washing powder? The same could be said about this whole urban landscape, long since transformed into a dual carriageway road. *C.Carter*

© Robert J. Harley 2023

First published 2023

ISBN 978 1 85414 482 9

Published by Heathfield Publishing in Heathfield, East Sussex

Printed by Parksons Graphics

CONTENTS

Introduction and Acknowledgements		4
1.	Driver and Conductor	8
2.	Sunlight and Shade	22
3.	Trams: Banquo's Ghost at the Feast	32
4.	North to South	36
5.	Landmarks, Junctions and Termini	43
6.	Riding the 16/18	52
7.	The Man on the Clapham Tram	59
Appendices		
A.	Julian Thompson's Tramway Diary 1949-51	66
B.	Extract from *John Bull* magazine, 23 September 1950	78
C.	London Trams in Colour	81
Bibliography		96

Introduction and Acknowledgements

My own introduction to trams began in the spring of 1952, when the Harley household moved to within walking distance of Well Hall Road, Eltham. Like most Londoners we were reliant on public transport. From our local stop by the Welcome Inn tram routes 46 and 72 headed into the centre of town. Suburban shopping trips took us to Woolwich and Lewisham; short working service 44 linked Eltham and Beresford Square, Woolwich.

These journeys left a lasting impression; however, my pleasure was short lived. That summer London joined the ranks of other British cities, which had abandoned their tramways in favour of buses.

After the tramlines were ripped up, the street landscape changed for ever. The legacy bequeathed by the trams to South London faded, but stubbornly remained at certain locations. A trip along the old 68/70 route prompted my father, who was a civil engineer, to talk about the post war reconstruction of Deptford Creek lifting bridge complete with new tram tracks, a fact he considered a total waste of money. He became one of many motorists certain that the demise of the 'railbound menace' would ease traffic conditions. He turned out to be wrong, as did almost all the other town planners.

In response to readers' requests, especially those from senior citizens, the balance of this book is firmly on the illustrative side with less emphasis on blocks of text and technical details of the tram fleet. Inevitably in a book dealing with the post-war years, the focus is on South London; in any case the spiritual home of the London tram. In order to recreate a lost era I have chosen the work of contemporary photographers, in particular Don Thompson. He sought to capture the working world of South London, and in so doing he preserved the character of the trams in their traditional setting, now long lost. In the intervening decades whole communities have been rendered extinct. Sensitive restoration of local landmarks was never on the agenda, once the 'urban renewal experts' of the second half of the twentieth century were given free rein.

Don told me that while other more famous and fashionable photographers sang the praises of 'the light and the fog' as they focussed on tourist landmarks and the financial quarter of the City of London, he preferred fine weather to take pictures. To him the trams looked their best when the sun was out.

The illustrations in this book set the scene of a capital city recovering from the devastation of the Blitz. In 1952 many people looked forward to a 'Second Elizabethan Age' of modernity which, they were told, had no place for the tramcar. Other folk were less impressed by the abandonment programme, where higher fares coupled with pollution in the form of exhaust fumes from large numbers of diesel buses did not sound such an appealing prospect.

Contributors to this book describe experiences in their own words. In quoting from extensive correspondence and personal interviews I wish to record my thanks to friends and fellow members of the Tramway and

Light Railway Society (TLRS) and the former Light Railway Transport League (LRTL). I am particularly grateful to John Barrie, John Meredith, Gerald Druce, Julian Thompson, Alan Watkins, John Gillham, John Wills, Roy Hubble, John Price, John Prentice, Dave Jones of the LCC Tramways Trust, Colin Withey, Eddie Dawes, Bob Appleton, David Voice, Vic Mitchell and Clarence Carter. Mike Eyre processed the colour pictures; Online Transport Archive gave access to photos taken by John Meredith.

Special mentions go to Hugh Taylor for his support in supplying photographs and to Jim Whiting for his wise advice and encouragement in completing this project.

Robert J Harley
Heathfield, July 2023

The London tramcar in all its splendour. Imagine the reaction of a motorist with this vehicle looming in the rear view mirror! UCC Feltham car 2094 on an enthusiasts' special tarries awhile in the afternoon sunshine. South London suburbia looks its best. *Alan Watkins*

Spring time at Victoria after a passing April shower. In contrast to the Feltham, car 1956 presents a more orthodox general shape, resembling hundreds of other vehicles in the fleet. The passenger loading islands at this location were particularly useful in shifting people safely during the morning and evening rush hours. *Alan Watkins*

Unfortunately, time travel has yet to be invented, thus we are unable to stand at this stop in Plumstead to await the arrival of our transport of choice. In this July 1952 scene car 186 glides past the external wall of the Royal Arsenal, Woolwich. When this tram reaches Abbey Wood, the landscape will be greener and more countrified. *Roy Hubble*

LONDON
TRAM
TRANSPORT
STOP
BY REQUEST
TRAMWAYS
TROLLEY
BUS
REQUEST
STOP
36

1 Driver and Conductor

Too often the people who actually ran the show at street level get neglected. So we begin by looking at the men and women who kept the wheels turning. Their employer the London Passenger Transport Board had metamorphosed on 1st January 1948 into the London Transport Executive with its headquarters at 55 Broadway S.W.1. Transport policy was firmly in favour of ridding the capital of its remaining tramways as circumstances permitted in the austerity years after the Second World War.

Each tramcar had a crew of two. The main duties of the driver or motorman were to regulate the speed of the vehicle and to judge when to apply the brakes. He was in charge of piloting the 'old gal' through the streets - all trams were referred to as 'she'. As motor traffic increased during the post war years the task of the man at the controls became more onerous.

John Barrie spent many an hour observing the public transport scene here at the end of Holloway Road by the Archway Tavern. In the distance a 609 trolleybus turns right into Archway Road. Overhead wires lead straight ahead to Highgate Hill. The facing crossover in front of car 1934 was sometimes used to turn trams short if there was a snarl up at the road junction. Note the J Lyons' Corner House with the elaborate façade, where you could get a good cup of tea and a decent snack in post war years. *Don Thompson*

Opposite the Crown and Anchor pub in Woolwich we catch up with car 168, allegedly the fastest in the fleet - pictured here at rest, definitely not exceeding the 30 mph speed limit! This location at Market Hill features the changeover point where the conduit commenced; the conductress is about to reach for the rope to haul the trolley pole down in readiness for the trip to central London. *Don Thompson*

The conductor collected the fares and gave out the tickets. He or she also kept a watchful eye out on passengers, especially as they boarded or alighted at stops. Both driver and conductor had to possess some mechanical knowledge in order to cope with the conduit method of current collection and generally to fix problems on the road. Bearing in mind the age of some of their charges - trams were renowned for their longevity - the crew belonged to a versatile and resourceful elite of London Transport workers.

John Barrie formed a life long affection for tramways in the 1930s after observing the workings of his local routes in North London and Middlesex. For him it was a painful process to attend so many 'last tram nights' as services were replaced by trolleybuses. After the war he concentrated his attentions on the routes which ran from Holloway Depot, north to south via the Kingsway Subway. In the late 1990s from his home in Seaton, Devon, John wrote to your author about life on the trams in the 1950s:

'...During the last two years of tramway operation in London there were approximately 750 cars in daily service working out of nine depots. The tramway abandonment plan had just been announced and it had been decided to convert the whole of the tramway system to diesel buses instead of trolleybuses, and it was anticipated that London would be clear of trams by the end of 1952 with the trolleybuses following at a later date.

At this well known spot car 169 is pictured on the Westminster Bridge tracks, which were positioned to the northern side of the carriageway. Two classic London black taxis appear to be racing to get to the other side of the Thames. This is strange, because many of us South Londoners reckoned our neck of the woods was *terra incognita* for cabbies, who preferred to stay put in the West End and other affluent parts! On the south side of the river it was better to stick to the trams; the fares were cheaper. *Don Thompson*

The past meets the present in this study of ex-Croydon Corporation car 399 as it traverses the single track on the corner of George Street by the historic Whitgift Almshouses. At the time this picture was taken in 1951, few could have foreseen that half a century later trams would be running across from George Street as part of London Tramlink. Note the Saturday morning shoppers the splendid 1931 Vauxhall Cadet with the London registration. *C. Carter*

Three members of London Transport staff combine to ensure car 1910 leaves Purley Depot safely. Traffic is sparse on the Brighton Road, so one wonders why all three were necessary. Service 42 was the local Croydon route and had been worked by Purley Depot since rebuilding of Thornton Heath Depot had commenced on 1st January 1950. *Don Thompson*

The tram and trolleybus section of the undertaking had amalgamated with the bus section a couple of years previously and all now came under the control of Central Road Services with head offices at 55 Broadway under the management of Mr J.B.Burnell. The divisional offices for the trams were at Camberwell for the South Eastern Division, Vauxhall for the South Western and at Manor House for the Northern. There were several recruiting centres over the combine, including medical centres and training schools. The tram driving school was situated at Clapham.

After the war there was a large influx of new recruits, many of them taking up employment after being demobbed from the army, and also staff who had previously worked on the trams were returning from war service. At the same time female staff were also being recruited at all depots with the exception of Norwood, but women were never permitted to take over as tram drivers.

Post war staff found great improvements in working conditions compared with those that had existed before the war and staff were now treated as human beings. Discipline still had to be strict, but the inhumanity of the pre war years had gone. Staff no longer had to drive open fronted tramcars and the working week had been reduced to 44 hours. No duty now exceeded eight hours actual working and had to include at least a 40 minute meal break. Spread over duties now had to be paid for and Saturday and Sunday duties now attracted enhanced payments.

Duties ran from Sunday to Saturday alternating between early and late shifts. The pay week ran from Wednesday to Tuesday with one rest day, which ran progressively one day forward, thus when the rest day was Tuesday for one week it could be Wednesday the following week, which meant that every seven weeks staff had two rest days in succession.

After recruits had finally passed out at the training school, they were allocated to a home depot usually as near as possible to where they lived. Conductor instructors received two shillings on top of their weekly wage when they accompanied a trainee on a regular duty. Staff initially went on to the Spare List where they would be allocated to any vacant duties covering leave, sickness etc. They would however be allocated to a service on a seniority basis as soon as one arose.

Spare staff also covered the rest day duties, but in the case of Holloway Depot this was not possible, as no driver with less than six months experience was allowed to drive through the Kingsway Subway. As Holloway had no other tram routes for drivers to gain the necessary six months experience, rest days had to covered by service staff. Thus four extra duties were inserted into the roster where staff spent a week covering the rest days on the roster. These weeks were known as 'dummy' weeks.

Each tram carried a running number on the side of the car which indicated the position of the car in the service. Numbers went from 1 upwards; unlike buses the trams did not carry a depot code. The only way that the depot could be identified was from the duty number on the side of the conductor's ticket box. Extra trams were inserted into the service during peak times and these carried running numbers continuing on from the highest service number. These cars were known as 'swingers'.

The driver of car 1908 uses his initiative and skill to pilot his charge through this melee of motor traffic. Here in Brixton there is a loading island for northbound trams; however, potential passengers for Streatham and beyond have to take their lives in their hands. RT3981 on tramway replacement service route 57 attempts to get ahead of his railbound rival. *Don Thompson*

The sun doesn't always shine; sometimes the tram crews had to battle the elements as here at Manor House, terminus of service 33. Whilst rubber tyred traffic had to take it carefully, the trams were on surer footing. In fact they could be relied upon to turn up in all weathers including the infamous 'pea souper' London fogs. Don Thompson

Each depot had its own system of working the rosters. In the case of the larger depots such as New Cross staff were allocated to a group of routes, but in the case of the smaller depots they rotated around all routes. Certain routes however such as those which traversed Dog Kennel Hill, the Kingsway Subway and service 34, drivers had to have more than six months experience. They were kept on a separate roster.

On booking on for duty the conductor would ask for his ticket box which would be, say, No 6 on the Subways; he would then find out from the allocation board which tram he would have to take. He would then find his driver and off they would go after having sorted out his tickets and of course the inevitable cup of tea in the canteen. Tickets on the Kingsway Subway routes were divided into 'A Type' going south and 'B Type' going north. Change over between the two groups occurred at Forest Hill for service 35.

Holloway Depot had the most complex fare structure imaginable and it was necessary for a conductor to carry two ticket racks to accommodate all the different tickets. A different ticket was issued for each direction of travel. Spare conductors drawn from the trolleybus staff were absolutely petrified about working the Subway routes, as well as the complicated fare structure with all the different transfer fares, they were working in a territory with which they were not familiar. They were also not used to trams and were unfamiliar with such duties as applying the hand brake at termini, replacing blown out breakers switches and having to change points in the middle of the road. As a result it was always possible for the tram enthusiast conductors who were spare conductors to volunteer to do all tram duties and thus not ever to work on the trolleybuses.

Unlike the bus section duties could be performed on two different routes on the same day, thus a Holloway duty might consist of a 'rounder' (as one complete round trip was known) on the 35s and a rounder on the 33s.

Tram work was much more congenial than the buses. The conductor had more space to move around and was not slung all over the place as on a bus. Then there was always the inevitable jug of tea. Many of the duties on the trams did not include stand time at the terminus as did the buses. The only stand time on some duties that was allocated, was what the driver could gain by using top notch. In the case of the Embankment circular routes there was no way that stand time could be had at the London end, which meant that in the case of Abbey Wood drivers they had to do Abbey Wood round to Abbey Wood without any break. The coffee jug routine was for the conductor to jump off the car at the recognised coffee shop and deposit his jug which was then picket up steaming hot on the return journey. Try balancing a full jug in the cab of any bus or trolleybus!

For some unknown reason tram passengers always seemed more congenial than those on the buses, perhaps it was because they were not being shaken about so much. There always seemed to be a much better relationship between crew and passenger. One of the aspects of the job that made life pleasanter for the tram driver was that he was not shut away isolated in his cab and could always have a chat with his conductor, or if the front door was open in the summer, he was also in contact with his passengers.

The most envied drivers of course were those out of Telford Avenue Depot with the Felthams. Here the driver had a nice warm cab, a seat and air brakes. They were the only London trams (apart from LCC no.1) fitted with heaters. Unfortunately owing to rather poor maintenance standards these fine cars were never shown to their full advantage and always looked rather battered and run down.

There also seemed to be a much better comradeship between tram crews than on the buses. Employees were issued with a free travel pass. Called a 'sticky' by the crews, the facility did not apply to spouses. However, such was the esprit de corps amongst tramway men and women that conductors would not charge the partner. Indeed, platform staff benefited from a first class relationship with their regulars, particularly office cleaners, charladies, printers, newspaper workers and Fleet Street journalists. Early morning and late night runs encouraged their own form of camaraderie.

Tram crews did not indulge in the habit of trying to get the chap in front to pick up the passengers whilst sitting on his tail. There was of course always the black sheep and you would get the odd driver out who would perpetually drag the road (go slow) in order to run late, which meant being turned back short of his destination.

Tram working was much more flexible than that of the buses and seemed to work more for the benefit of the passengers. Regulators who were posted at intervals along the length of the route would deal with the actual running of the trams and would have the power to turn a car back where necessary to cover a gap in the service, or even divert them to another route to cover a gap. That was of course provided the driver was familiar with the diversion.

Inspectors were posted to a section of route and they used to deal with ticketing matters, such as passengers not paying the proper fare or conductors who were not issuing the correct ticket. In the latter days of the trams a much more human relationship existed between the supervisory staff and the platform staff; there was no room for the 'little Hitlers' of pre war days. It was always beneficial for regulators to cooperate with crews as situations arose where a favour was required such as unofficial overtime or having to detram passengers. In return these officials could always repay any favour at a later convenient time by giving the crew a chance to finish their duty early.

As I have mentioned, working on the trams in the post war years was a vastly different experience to pre war. Pre war days one was expected to drive an open fronted tramcar for up to 9 hours without a break. Crews were expected to work anywhere on the system, finishing up at say Holloway at midnight on Saturday, and be expected to be at Clapham first thing on Sunday. How they made their way was their problem!

After the war they were at least treated like human beings. However, owing to the fact that it was now much easier to find employment, staff were no longer willing to put up with low pay and shift work. The consequence was a constant turnover of staff and sometimes a deterioration in discipline. The maintenance standard of the trams dropped owing to the difficulty of keeping up with the arrears of repairs caused by the war years. It was necessary to lower the standards expected of a tram driver.

One of the commonest faults with newer drivers (many of whom were ex servicemen) was that they got over confident and tended not to keep their distance from the vehicle in front. This was the reason for the increasing number of two car collisions, plus the fact that the cars had no adequate braking system in the event of a failure of the magnetic brakes. Most of these accidents were only of a minor nature, but the press made great play about 'dangerous tramcars'. As far as serious accidents were concerned, the trams still maintained a very high safety record.

On the North Side (Holloway Depot) things were much better, as the trams were only driven by senior men who had many years of experience, which was necessary to be allowed to drive through the Kingsway Subway. That is not to say they used to hang around and most of them could put a tram through its paces, knowing how to get maximum speed, but in the right locations. It is well known how on depot bound journeys there was always an extra notch that mysteriously could always be found.

Conductor Harry Ellis, a chap I knew, told me that one evening on the run from the Subway along Theobalds Road the cabby tailing them informed the driver that he had clocked them at 45 mph. This was no mystery to the tram staff, as the vehicle concerned was car 168, the star performer of the post war fleet. Together with car 173 the two could show a clean pair of heals to any bus or trolleybus working along the same road.

Much more could be said about working on the trams. For many they were really happy days and the majority of the crews did not really look forward to working on the buses. When that last tram ran into New Cross Depot it was a sad day for all and the job just went to pot....'

The Operating Department Trams And Trolleybuses to use the full official title, issued this handbook of 195 pages, which attempted to cover every eventuality in the operational life of the staff. Not only did drivers and conductors have to cope with passengers and other road users, but they also had to possess a good mechanical knowledge of their trams. This particular copy of the Rule Book belonged to an experienced driver at Holloway Depot, probably known to John Barrie. E.H. Broad was a skilled motorman trained to operate the Kingsway Subway services that ran across the capital from north to south.

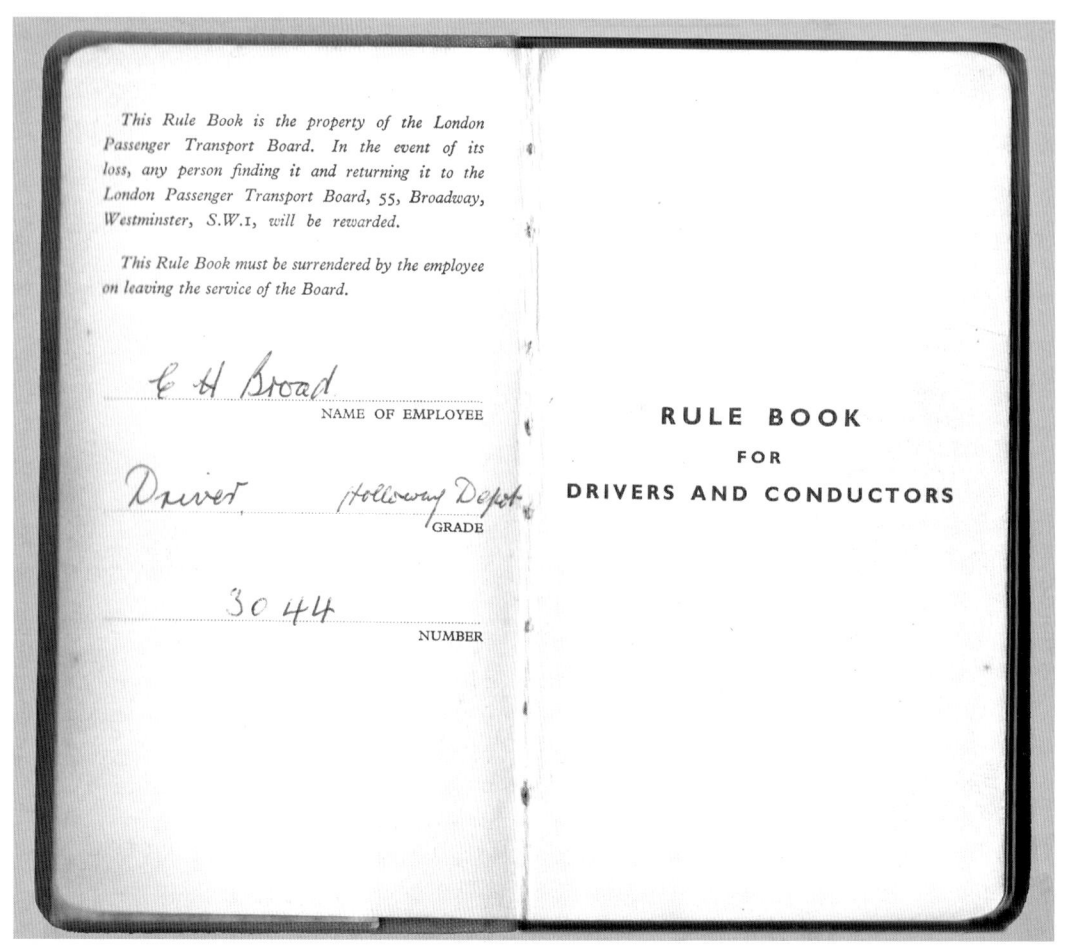

On the last day it is fair to say rules were bent to accommodate joy riders and special tours filled with enthusiasts. In a lively conversation between staff one wonders if they are discussing strategies to get through to the evening with their wits intact! The driver of a passing bus (RT1864) had opened his cab door to contribute his two pennyworth. This bus is working route 109 in replacement of tram services 16/18.

Correspondence from Julian Thompson (no relation to Don), a keen observer of the London tramway scene, casts more light on the wages and fares of the period:

'....A tram crew worked an average of 65 miles per day, which meant about six and half hours on the road. For a 44 hour week starting wages were £5-16s (£5.80), rising to £6-5s (£6.25) after two years. Pay for crews did rise in the last two years of the trams and eventually reached parity with the busmen, who had always been paid more.

Just to add some context to the average wage, costs of two household staples were five pence (2p) for a loaf of bread and about the same for a pint of milk. Tea was under a shilling (5p) a packet. You had to be fairly comfortably off to own a car. It is fair to say most tram passengers would not have had the cash to splash out £500 or so for an Austin or one of the other British makes. Then you had to put fuel in it. I believe petrol was around three shillings (15p) a gallon (4.5 litres).

Eltham Hill once looked like this before it became a congested dual carriageway. Tackling the slope past the entrance to Prince John Road, car 166 makes progress towards Eltham High Street. To the right of the tram is one of the many inter war housing estates constructed by the London County Council in conjunction with the Metropolitan Borough of Woolwich. An efficient LCC tram service, giving cheap and reliable public transport, was part of the housing policy, before the Council lost control of the tramways in 1933. *Don Thompson*

Fares were remarkably stable during this period. The cost of riding London trams was reasonable, good value for the distances covered. Every conductor needed to possess a near encyclopaedic knowledge of all the transfers, workmen's tickets and other bargains on offer. As an example, anyone getting on a route 46 car at the northern end of Southwark Bridge (City terminus) could ride all the way to Beresford Square, Woolwich for 7d. In fact if this person so desired (perhaps he or she was a tram enthusiast) to remain onboard, a depot run out as far as Abbey Wood would not have added to the cost. The workmen's return fare between the City and Woolwich was only 8d (3p)!

Fares were adjusted in October 1950, with the disappearance of workmen's and return fares. You did not have to be a cynic to realise that tramway abandonment came at a cost in fare rises, which set a pattern for the rest of the decade. But then, we of the tramway fraternity had been warning about this for some time...'

In addition to distributing tickets to passengers, another useful service was supervised by the conductor. The London Transport Rule book states:

'....In the case of trams, accompanied luggage and parcels may be carried upon the Driver's platform, provided that it is not objectionable or dangerous or likely to impede the Driver in the performance of his duty. For such luggage, excluding folding perambulators, which may be carried free, a charge of 2d must be made in respect of each article or package carried on the front platform. An appropriate ticket must be punched and issued by the Conductor to the passenger and the label affixed to the luggage....'

Needless to say, this handy method of freight transport disappeared when diesel buses took over, much to the chagrin of market traders and Covent Garden flower sellers. Conductor David Profit of Holloway Depot remembered once having three crates of racing pigeons on the front platform of his tram. Sometimes you just had to wait for the right tram. Author and tramway expert, John Price, recalled the trouble he had attempting to convey the cadet corps' bass drum from Croydon to a repair shop in Kennington. He had to let three Felthams go by until an E/3 turned up. The drum was just too big for the Feltham's front door!

During the last week of trams in July 1952 many souvenir photos were taken. Rarely did the interior of the lower deck feature; however, we are fortunate to have this detailed shot of the lower saloon of car 187 at Southwark Bridge terminus. One assumes the conductor has gone to join the driver and will return to his post when they set off again to Beresford Square, Woolwich. Note the boys wearing their school caps. *Don Thompson*

It is easy to forget the capital once enjoyed the benefits of non polluting electric traction on its roads. Here at Plumstead we observe tramcar 1917 being pursued by trolleybus 788 on route 696 to Dartford. The dwellings to the right of the picture are typical of the local housing stock. In an era before central heating people relied on coal fires, which were inefficient in keeping the cold at bay. Dampness, restricted light and the risk of flooding affected the quality of life for residents living in the basement. *Don Thompson*

An animated scene in Blackwall Lane features trolley less HR/2 car 149 as it passes Lenthorpe Road. Sandwiched between the tram and the lorry is a bus on Blackwall Tunnel route 108. Photographer Don Thompson had a knack of capturing a sunny interlude, just before the rain clouds rolled in. Note the pedestrian crossing yet to receive the familiar zebra stripes. *Don Thompson*

The tracks along the Victoria Embankment were a favoured spot for photographers. Before the post war abandonment got going in September 1950, we view car 161 at John Carpenter Street. It is about to attempt the "round the 'ouses" service 34, ending up in Beaufort Street, Chelsea by the well known Kings Road. On 17th March 1950, Battersea Bridge was damaged and all traffic was curtailed to a point south of the structure. The tramway to Chelsea was then abandoned. *Don Thompson*

2 Sunlight and Shade

Although urban landscapes characterised South London, the sea of houses was also punctuated with parks and green spaces. Gaps in the streets caused by the Blitz added to the variety. Derelict sites had been colonised by wild flowers and bushes, particularly Buddleia. Artists and authors, who believed rather romantically the streets of South London only revealed their true nature when veiled in rain or shrouded in fog, probably lived somewhere else.

As a native tucked away in the south eastern quarter of the metropolis, your author can testify the climate was not always inclement. In the spring we looked forward to the sun appearing after a passing April shower. Everywhere sparkled; the tramlines glistened like slivers of silver. On balmy summer's days the red and cream tramcars ran through corridors formed by roadside rows of London plane trees in full leaf. At one particular location on Eltham Road between Kidbrooke Park Road and Lee Green overarching trees created a tunnel almost three quarters of a mile long.

The trams gave great value. Leaving the hustle and bustle of the city behind, a cheap family excursion to the countryside started at Abbey Wood terminus, a short walk away from the ruins of the twelfth century Lesnes Abbey and the surrounding woods. A reliable service appealed to regular passengers on the way to their place of work; at times of bad weather, such as snow and fog, the dedication to duty of tramway workers came to the fore. Drivers and conductors rejected the idea of staying in the depot and waiting for the tempest to pass. They were a hardy bunch!

On the other side of the coin the enjoyment of a tram ride felt by many ordinary Londoners was not shared by the powers that be. Storm clouds were gathering. It appeared to the dwindling band of tram lovers that the government and the public transport establishment deliberately and unfairly denigrated the objects of their desire. Experts had spoken from 55 Broadway S.W.1. Buses could do a better job, they opined.

The London Transport people were joined by hostile journalists intent on twisting the knife. According to their reports, trams never went anywhere quietly. They 'clanked, groaned and screeched', allegedly making so much racket they were even demonised as the 'criminals' friend'. The sound of the night tram in Southwest London was said to mask the activities of smash and grab robbers.

As part of the prestigious County Books series, Harry Williams wrote the volume on South London. First published in 1949, the author wastes no words in giving his opinion on trams in the environment. Admittedly, his description of the former LCC Tramways power station on the banks of the Thames at Greenwich as a 'monster' rings true. However, we get the full flavour in the following passage:

Car 1884 on service 58 is depicted in Lordship Lane. There was greenery aplenty in this part of the Metropolitan Borough of Camberwell. In views like this the esthetic qualities of the conduit system came to the fore. An open skyline with no overhead wires added to the charm of a scene with oaks and elms in full leaf. *Don Thompson*

Here amongst the suburban villas of Abbey Wood, car 1999 demonstrates its versatility by reversing on a conveniently placed crossover. Note the London Plane trees, which, according to the fashion of the 1950s, have been pollarded. Overhead wires also accommodate the 698 trolleybus route that outlasted the trams in this area by less than seven years. Passengers wait by the roadside to board on the journey back to New Cross, while the conductress on the rear platform attends to the handbrake handle. *Don Thompson*

Author Harry Williams found little to please him in the South London streetscape. By the entrance to Greenwich South Street this cameo must have escaped his attention. Car 133 on service 58 loads passengers for the journey to the centre of Greenwich and the terminus at the southern portal of Blackwall Tunnel. Note the wealth of period detail. The Coach & Horses pub, the café and the Royal Arsenal Cooperative Society grocers on the corner of Blackheath Hill (the A2, Watling Street) all cater for local workers. Single track and passing loops characterised this section of route 58. There were no signals. Tram drivers relied on line of sight for safe passage. *Don Thompson*

'....South London street by street...the pattern is almost always the same, a relentless repetition of dirty pub rubbing shoulders with dirty pub, poor little shops standing cheek by jowl with poor little shops, miles upon miles of silver ribboned tramlines, heralding the passing of rocking juggernauts along miles upon miles of ill lighted, monotonous thoroughfares, over and over again.....the soul of man is being killed under such conditions....'

The last comment sounds extreme. One wonders why poor Mr Williams took on the task of writing the book in the first place, when his sensibilities were so offended by the landscape of inner South London. However, even when the author arrives in the leafy suburbs of Eltham the critique continues:

'....the roads have an appearance of indecision, as though unaware of their ultimate destination. Roundabouts, petrol stations, shops, schools, public houses and the everlasting forest of tramway posts are dotted here and there....'

Thus, the charm of small shops, pubs with painted signs, roads paved with granite setts, the ubiquitous London Plane trees, the variety of traffic, motorised or horse drawn, and the traders shouting their wares in the street markets served by the ever present trams failed to make any sort of positive impression on Mr Williams.

In deference to Harry Williams he, like many of his contemporaries, was smitten by the County of London Plan of 1943. Nowadays we would say he had 'bought into' the vision promoted by Messrs Forshaw and Abercrombie, the report's authors. Full of glossy illustrations, maps and diagrams, the 188 page volume set the tone for years to come. However, unfortunately for town planning futurists, nobody seemed to have predicted that a near bankrupt country after the World War would not be able to afford grandiose schemes such as ring roads and deep level underground railway lines.

Paragraph 203 of the County of London Plan states:

'....Having in mind the fact that trams were to have been removed from the roads by 1943, we have assumed, in preparing this Report, that they will be replaced by other means of transportation at an early date after the war. Such a removal will contribute in no small way to the reduction in casualty figures....'

This last line was peddling the myth that trams on London's streets were inherently dangerous - a convenient stick with which to beat the older, railbound form of transport. Most accidents were caused by reckless motorists intimidating passengers boarding and alighting. With one or two exceptions London Transport had singularly failed to provide loading islands or pedestrian safety zones at tram stops.

The change pit at Lee Green was situated at the start of the 'green tunnel' that was Eltham Road. Car 1859 squeezes past the Bowaters lorry inbound from Kent. It is probably loaded with reels of paper. In the foreground car 1936 waits for the conduit plough to be inserted. The poster on the side of the tram announces LAST TRAM WEEK. Most of the track and tramway infrastructure at this location was lifted in the late spring of 1953.

Car 593 crosses the north side of Clapham Common, one of the 'green lungs' of the capital, on a fine day in the summer of 1950. Trams at this location formed a backdrop to one of the scenes in the 1944 film *This Happy Breed*, which was shot in colour. *Don Thompson*

Southwark Bridge terminus actually lay within the confines of the City of London, which was feat in itself, considering the authorities in this affluent part of the world had suffered from tram phobia since the nineteenth century! In bright sunshine car 1145 heads the queue, while two members of the central red bus fleet - RT721 (JXC 84) on route 18B and STD34 (DLU 344) on route 13 - pass on the other side. *Don Thompson*

Lordship Lane in the S.E.22 Postal District was largely a bus free zone, where the trams were unencumbered by motor traffic. The photographer is fortunate in capturing the moment when cars 104 and 154 passed one another. On a technical note, neither vehicle possessed a trolley pole, so they were confined to conduit equipped routes only. *Don Thompson*

Thomas Street, Woolwich, a location well known to your author on account of shopping trips by tram from Eltham. It could be early closing Thursday, because some of the smaller shops are shuttered. Car 87 only has a few days of active life ahead before the axe falls and service 46 is replaced by bus route 182. *Don Thompson*

Contemporary cuttings reveal some of the morbid fascination local and national newspapers had for tram accidents. Some journalists decided it was good copy for their readers. Of course it was unfair. Sadly there were plenty of other traffic collisions in the metropolitan area which did not feature. Usually each conversion stage of the abandonment programme occupied column space, often written in a nostalgic tone.

TWO HURT IN TRIPLE CRASH

(1103)

NO. 34 TRAM, A BUS AND LORRY COLLIDE

"*Evening News*" Reporter

TWO people were injured to-day when a tram, a lorry and a bus were involved in a collision in Coldharbour-lane, Brixton.

The tram, a No. 34, was on its way to Chelsea. Both the tram and the lorry were badly damaged, but the bus was only slightly damaged.

Mr. P. R. Connell, of Thorne-

The damaged tram

road, South Lambeth, the tram driver, is detained in King's College Hospital. Mr. J. Willis, of Camberwell-road, Camberwell, a passenger on the tram, sustained bruises and shock.

Trolley Arm Smash

Several passengers in a No. 679 trolley-bus, on its way to Waltham Cross, had narrow escapes from injury by flying glass to-day in Upper-street, Islington.

The overhead arm of another trolley left the wires, broke a street lamp, and smashed a window on the top deck.

The passengers were transferred to another trolley, and the damaged bus was taken out of service.

565

Tramcars crash—five injured

Five passengers received minor injuries in a collision between two London-bound tramcars on the 46 route at Well Hall Road, Eltham, soon after 9 a.m. to-day.

They were: Private Reginald Cameron, attached to the Royal Herbert Hospital, Shooters Hill; Mrs. Ethel Gill, of Dunblane Road, Eltham; Miss Dorothy Daynes, 38, of Arsenal Road, Eltham; Mrs. Jane Spinks, 31, of Bastion Road, Abbey Wood, and her three-year-old son John.

The track was blocked for 93 minutes. Routes 46 and 44 were affected.

Buses for Trams

The first stage in the replacement of London's trams by buses takes place on October 1.

Six routes and one all-night route will be concerned. In the table below, the existing tram routes are shown in light lettering and the bus routes by which they will be replaced in heavy lettering.

Route No.	Route
12	Wandsworth to Borough
44	**Mitcham to London Bdge.**
612	Mitcham to Battersea
44	**Mitcham to London Bdge.**
*26	Clapham Junction to Borough
†168	**Wandsworth to Farringdon Street**
28	Clapham Junction to Victoria Station
169	**Clapham Junction to Victoria Station**
31	Wandsworth to Islington
170	**Wandsworth to Hackney**
34	Chelsea to Blackfriars
***45**	**South Kensington Station to Farringdon Street**
3 ALL NIGHT	Battersea to Blackfriars
288 ALL NIGHT	**Wandsworth to Farringdon Street**

Tram route 72 will be extended from Savoy Street to Borough, to replace route 26 on this section.

Route 45 will operate as far as Battersea Garage only, until the re-opening of Battersea Bridge.

† *All night service.*

The new bus services will use the same roads as those now used by trolleybuses or trams but certain routes will be extended to meet traffic needs. Buses on Route 170 will run from Rosebery Avenue via Clerkenwell Road, Old Street, Hackney Road, Cambridge Heath Road and Mare Street.

Details of any of the new services will gladly be given by the Traffic Enquiry Office at 55 Broadway, Westminster, S.W.1 (Telephone: ABBEY 1234).

First of the scrapped trams starts off the bonfire at Charlton today.

100,000 WILL SWITCH TO BUSES

40 MILES OF TRAM LINES TO END

LONDON TRANSPORT officials are working at top pressure in readiness for the first big stage of the scrapping of London's tram system which takes place next Saturday.

Forty miles of routes serving nearly 100,000 passengers daily will be made ready for buses over the week-end. The trams will disappear from the streets at midnight and new bus services will be running over the routes early on Sunday morning.

The changeover is the first of nine stages spread over two years, in which the complete abolition of London trams will be brought about.

Routes Affected

These are the routes involved in next Saturday's change-over:
Tram route 12 (Wandsworth, Battersea, Vauxhall, and London Bridge) and Trolley-bus route 612 (Mitcham, Tooting, and Battersea) will be replaced by a new bus route 44 (Mitcham to London Bridge Station).
Tram Route 26 (Clapham Junction, Vauxhall, Westminster Bridge, Embankment and London Bridge) will be replaced by a new bus Route 168 (Wandsworth to Farringdon-street).
Tram Route 28 (Clapham Junction, Vauxhall and Victoria) will be replaced by new bus Route 169, covering the same route.
Tram Route 31 (Wandsworth, Battersea, Vauxhall, Westminster, Embankment, Bloomsbury and Islington Green) will be replaced by a new bus Route 170 (Wandsworth to Hackney Garage).
Tram Route 34 (Chelsea, Clapham, Camberwell, Elephant & Castle and Blackfriars) will be replaced by a new bus Route 45 (South Kensington to Farringdon-street).

"Star" Reporter

IN the "graveyard" of London's unwanted trams today Edward Greener—himself a regular tram passenger—obeyed a signal from London Transport officials and set fire to a 30-year-old tram of the former 28 route which on Saturday was carrying passengers between Clapham Junction and Victoria.

This tram, which had a history of one and a half million miles on London tram tracks, and had taken many thousands of pounds in fares, was one of 74 which London Transport is reducing to scrap by fire.

Fire is the only way to get rid of the woodwork economically so that the scrap—steel, iron and copper in the frame—can be separated and resold.

Glass, electric light fittings and other things are salvaged first.

At the rate of one a day the 73 other trams will be reduced to scrap by the same method. They come from routes 12, 26, 28, 31 and 34.

A further 23 trams, the modern Feltham type, from these routes have been sold to Leeds at £500 each.

The 28 tram, which was burned today, arrived with a posy of flowers on it, the last tribute from its crew.

Fireman E. Crick stood by with a hosepipe in case the fire might spread. "Sixty minutes is about the time it takes," said Mr Crick.

30

Opposite top: One near miss that failed to make the newspaper headlines was this encounter between car 1915 and a builder's lorry. The driver of the latter just about judged the gap to the last inch! Note the small newsagent/tobacconist shop so typical of this era. Advertising posters extol the virtues of *Woman's Companion*, *The Gardening Smallholder* and *Men Only*. Reflecting 1950s sensibilities, this men's magazine would have been displayed under a plain wrapper on the top shelf of the shop. *John Meredith*

Opposite: We observe a spot of bother at the Elephant and Castle. What exactly has happened to car 1406 is a mystery, although driver and inspector appear to have spied something amiss in the narrow space between tramcars. There is no actual evidence of accident damage, so the bus may just have come to a halt awkwardly without striking the tram. One theory is that car 1406 may be stuck on a dead section of the conduit. *John Wills*

Above: Camberwell Green was a tram spotter's paradise. Since the publication in 1948 of *ABC of London's Transport - No.2 Trams and Trolleybuses* by Ian Allan of Vauxhall Bridge Road, S.W.1, juvenile and not so young enthusiasts could cross off fleet numbers of vehicles they saw. With a maximum number of 250 trams passing in one hour, this was a favoured location. HR/2 class car 1897 heads for Victoria. *Don Thompson*

3 Trams: Banquo's Ghost at the Feast

Much has been written about the 1951 Festival of Britain. It has been lauded as one of the most significant cultural events in recent British history. After the dark years of the Second World War and the Blitz, the Festival gave Britons and especially Londoners a glimpse of a bright future, a time to wonder at the marvels of modern science, which would make life easier.

The tourist industry, such as it was in those days, went into overdrive. London Transport realised the value of advertising its services. Special routes were planned to connect the South Bank main site with Battersea Pleasure Gardens. Visitors were encouraged to patronise the tubes and buses. To ease traffic on the eastern side of Westminster Bridge at its junction with York Road a new one way scheme was projected.

My father once told me that in the late 1940s and early 1950s he and his colleagues had more than enough work in England supervising tram track removal and highway reconstruction. Rails were then carted away to the scrap merchant. However, he and the rest of the office read the *Contract Journal* in disbelief, when firms were asked to tender for roads in connection with the Festival, plus new conduit tram track and points. As he said, civil engineers looked at the date to check it wasn't 1st April!

Indeed, the government and just about everyone involved in creating the 1951 festivities appeared somewhat embarrassed by the continued presence of the trams. According to one unnamed official at 55 Broadway they haunted the scene like 'Banquo's Ghost at the Feast'. Fortunately, a salvo of Shakespeare quotes from members of the Light Railway Transport League in defence of their favourite form of transport failed to materialise. But the reality of the situation had to be faced. The powers that be were not in a position at that time to junk the rest of the network and go all bus. The proposed gyratory traffic scheme required new tramway infrastructure.

When construction got going, it acted like a magnet for the enthusiast fraternity. Included among them was Julian Thompson, who paid regular visits to the road works in order to document the progress of rail laying. Armed with a hand held board, plus drawing paper and pencils, his layout sketches drew a polite response from passers by. Seated at his small folding chair, Julian's presence prompted questions from members of the public, who were quite astonished that anyone would go to such lengths in the quest for accuracy. After all the old trams were on their way out, so everyone had been told. (Julian's on site diagrams are included with his 1949-1951 diary in Appendix A).

Interruptions to the tram service on Victoria Embankment occurred between 14th and 16th July, 19th and 21st August 1950. The cause was construction work on a Bailey Bridge across the Thames. It enabled pedestrians to gain access to the Festival site. The trams coped by running shuttle services either side of the obstruction.

Preliminary work on the South Bank commenced in 1949 and in the next few months the new gyratory traffic scheme took shape. When news reached the public, there was some speculation among LRTL and TLRS members that the stretch of track linking Battersea Pleasure Gardens with Westminster Bridge would be retained for a special Festival tram service. Those who lived in hope should have learnt from experience. Contrary to rumour, no such arrangement would be contemplated by the management at 55 Broadway.

Meanwhile preparations were going ahead in the London Transport publicity department. In a joint venture with British Railways a free folding map and guide was planned in order to inform visitors of the relevant public transport facilities serving the area.

In the best London Transport tradition of graphic design this portable sign was to be found on the Embankment during the couple of days' disruption, caused by the construction of the new temporary bridge across the river. Unfortunately the effect is rather mitigated by the sheets of newspaper on the ground. *Alan Watkins*

UCC Feltham car 2093 does the honours on the Embankment shuttle. A 1950s portable bollard, property of the Metropolitan Police, acts as a warning to protect potential passengers from other traffic. Typical for this era, even on a fine summer's day, the women and children are smartly dressed. *Alan Watkins*

The date is 20th April 1950. Work is under way installing conduit tram track from York Road into Addington Street. Evidence of demolition is apparent on the right of this view. For those readers with broader tastes in public transport, on the opposite side of York Road bus G65 on route 76 is obliged to take avoiding action. Ropes and red flags suffice; no plastic traffic cones in those days! *John Meredith*

Anecdotal evidence suggests LTE and BR cartographers were instructed not to include any reference to tram routes in the vicinity of the Festival. One presumes this course of action was prompted by sheer unease at the continuing existence of the 'people's carriage'.

Londoners who lived on the remaining tram routes which served the South Bank never took the hint. They knew the cheapest and most reliable method of reaching the exhibition site. Shortly after the Festival of Britain opened on 4th May 1951 a group of residents was observed in an orderly queue at the Briset Road stop on Westhorne Avenue. In just over three-quarters of an hour trams on route 72, operating on a ten minute service interval, would take visitors to their destination and then home again in the evening. Questioned by a local newspaper reporter the general consensus was that the day's outing was a bargain not to be missed.

Rails to the right of them, rails to the left of them: New conduit tracks, supposedly the last ever manifestation of this type in the world, excited enthusiasts and permanent way aficionados. Many workers engaged on track work soon became friendly with the multitude of 'them tram enthusiastics' who were pointing cameras at them and their handiwork. It is fair to say the whole project represented the 'last hurrah' of the London system.

Former Croydon Corporation car 388 passes one of the entrances to Waterloo Station. The track on this part of Westminster Bridge Road has been excavated in preparation of connecting rails to Addington Street. On the left of the picture note the stylish workman's wheelbarrow and the mobile compressor. It is easy to miss the TRACK UP warning sign.
Alan Watkins

It is mid June 1950. A vintage cement mixer occupies the side adjacent to the recently opened York Road/Addington Street single track. All new tramway infrastructure was numbered, so that contractors could assemble the whole layout in the correct order. The pointwork in the foreground was regarded by some as a thing of beauty in its symmetry. *Alan Watkins*

4 North to South

The tram to trolleybus conversion scheme of the 1930s had failed to solve the increasingly intractable problem of running replacement vehicles through the Kingsway Subway. This accounted for the fact that routes 31, 33 and 35 (the only remaining odd numbered services on the network), which linked North London with the rest of the remaining system, stayed basically intact, whilst all the other tram services north of the Thames had disappeared.

Home News

KINGSWAY TRAM TUNNEL SHUT

A LAST CEREMONIAL JOURNEY

FROM OUR SPECIAL CORRESPONDENT

In a storming finish up the steep gradient from Holborn station to Theobald's Road, Bloomsbury, No. 185 of London's trams, with more than 100 people on board, emerged from the Kingsway subway at 12.30 a.m. yesterday to a round of cheers and "Auld Lang Syne" played by a kilted piper.

It was the last tram to carry passengers through the tunnel which was opened in 1906 and reconstructed for double-deck vehicles in 1930.

This marked the seventh stage in conversion of tram services to bus routes, leaving one final phase for the week-end of July 5-6. Norwood, Brixton, Forest Hill, Brockley, on the south side, Bloomsbury, Islington, Manor House, Highgate, on the north, have been added to the districts where trams no longer run. The line from Kennington Gate to Brixton station was the oldest portion of London's tramway system, opened in 1870 for horse-drawn double-deck vehicles.

SOUVENIRS COLLECTED

No. 185 was taken by Driver Alfred Keir from under Big Ben just after midnight and spent half-an-hour over a journey scheduled for eight minutes. It banged briskly along the Embankment but met with ceremonial delays at the southern entrance to the subway and at each station. Passengers had ample time to affix garlands or detach souvenirs while photographs were taken, albums signed, and handshakes given.

One surprise was to meet in the tunnel an antique motor-car, about the same age as the subway, which before anyone could stop it had been sacrilegiously driven down from Bloomsbury on the tram track. At Aldwych station No. 185 passed No. 173, a special car with the Mayor of Holborn, Mr. E. Ling Cooper, on the driver's platform and an official party inside. At Holborn, Mr. "Paddy" Walker, a retired inspector, had arrived to call for the last time "Take her away."

Each section of the abandoned lines honoured the occasion. As the last southbound tram on service 33 entered the borough of Lambeth it was joined by No. 197, a decorated special car containing the Mayor, Mrs. E. L. Boltz, with her party, and the two proceeded together to Norwood depôt. Bloomsbury gave an affectionate send-off to No. 184, the last tram to take passengers north of the subway to Highgate.

Few were in the streets to hear the familiar and endearing groans as 13 trams from Highgate depôt, returning one by one, stripped of boards and indicators, their panoply of service, took finally the curving plunge from Theobald's Road and began their run to the "graveyard" at Charlton, leaving behind them the padlocked gates of a thoroughfare which for 46 years has notably helped Londoners to get across their city, and for the future of which there is no plan.

** Picture on page 12.

What to do with a Tunnel

W. R. Paulson, "Evening News" Motoring Correspondent, wrote about the ending of the tram service through the Kingsway Tunnel. He asked: Anybody want a tunnel? Here, from our postbag, are some comments.

THE Kingsway Tunnel should be used as a road passenger transport museum. The L.T.E. have a number of historic vehicles tucked away at the back of their garage at Reigate. These could be put on view.—*Laurence J. Kohler*, Pendennis-road, Tottenham.

IF the station staircases at Aldwych and Holborn were converted into ramps, the result would be an almost perfect car-park, and at 2s. 6d. per car a day the revenue would be considerable.—*Harold A. Major*, York Mansions, Battersea Park, S.W.

... Kingsway Tunnel, far from being a "white elephant," is a tribute to the farsightedness of the designers. We could do with more subways to carry the traffic.—*J. Joyce*, Somerset-avenue, Raynes Park.

... The article on the tunnel is superficial and misleading. The number of passengers carried since the opening — around 300 million—is ignored, as is the revenue. Of course the tunnel is useless for motor traffic—it was designed for more precise and cleaner traffic.—*D. E. Shirley*, B.Sc., Crieff-road, S.W.18.

... Keep it as a tramway tunnel with a few selected routes and modern equipment.—*J. W. Fowler*, Light Railway Transport League, Cricklewood-broadway, N.W.

... Make it into an underground cinema. Then get all the American cowboy films ever made and lock film critic Jympson Harman in with them, making them run perpetually. That should make him change his mind about British producers.—"*Albert Embankment*" (name and address supplied).

Note: Suggestions of turning the tunnel into a car-park are being investigated. Chief difficulty is the narrowness and danger of fires in confined space. Its use for trams is to end in April—as part of the conversion-to-buses scheme.

Anybody want a Tunnel?

SIX experts in search of a use for the Kingsway Tunnel recently went for a motor ride. They took a car through the tunnel while the trams were safely tucked up for the night in their depots. Then they began calculating the cost of conversion and improvement.

It will take them some months yet to reach a conclusion on the future of the tunnel. But when the last trams rumble through on a Saturday night in April London Transport will say good-bye to the Kingsway Tunnel —and, as far as they are concerned good riddance.

For the tunnel is a white elephant, and for ordinary traffic would soon be a black sheep. Conceived in 1898, built in 1906 at a cost of no-one-knows-what, deepened in 1930 for £330,000 to take double-deckers and widened for another £70,000 at the Embankment approaches in 1936, it has had floods when a water main burst, gassed a couple of workmen who were repairing the sewer pipes below, and necessitated the constant attendance of a police officer and a tram guide to sort out the traffic hold-ups where trams turn across the Embankment.

IN 1930 the Metropolitan Police Commissioner summarised the objections to its use by motor traffic as the congestion which would arise at each end of the tunnel; the still worse traffic block which would quickly develop if one vehicle broke down inside; the danger of exhaust fumes among slow traffic, or even fire. The London Traffic Advisory Committee at that time recommended that the Kingsway Tunnel could serve no useful purpose as a motor-way, and the Transport Ministry, which accepted their advice, is hardly likely to alter that decision now

W. R. Paulson

After the war when the diesel bus was chosen to supplant the tramcar, the same old problems of steerable vehicles attempting to negotiate the narrow confines of the Subway defied the ingenuity of the best brains at London Transport.

The notion of retaining trams on this major traffic artery fell on stony ground. The idea was dismissed out of hand, without it appears any debate on a possible shortened, modified tram service linking Bloomsbury to the Victoria Embankment. The bus faction at 55 Broadway reigned supreme, with the result that on 5th April 1952 the last tramcars were withdrawn from the Kingsway Subway.

Before and after the trams took their leave there was speculation in the press about the future of the Subway. In November 1951 a committee was set up to explore alternative uses. These deliberations included an all expenses paid visit to Paris to study motor tunnels in the St Cloud district. Nothing substantial happened until the opening of the Strand Underpass on 21st January 1964, which involved the conversion into a road tunnel and the obliteration of Aldwych Tram Station. The section north of here including Holborn Station remained almost as it was in tramway days.

The structure has lasted the test of time. Conduit tracks on the ramp leading to the north portal by Southampton Row now have Grade II listed status, a monument to the folly of London Transport and to British 'short termism'.

The northern terminus of service 35 was close to Archway tube station. As can be seen from the trolleybus overhead wires, electric traction was well entrenched in this area. Car 118 was timetabled to reach Forest Hill in just under one hour and a half. Traversing the Kingsway Subway normally took around four minutes from Bloomsbury, Southampton Row to the stop on the Embankment in the shadow of Waterloo Bridge. The adult through fare was one shilling and three pence (7p).
Don Thompson

Having crossed London from north to south, car 176 is stationary on the terminal stub at Forest Hill. Noteworthy in this view are the typical parade of small shops and the carpet delivery van passing on the wrong side of the road. In the course of the day very little traffic disturbed this suburban backwater. The centre of the suburb by Forest Hill Station was served by tram routes 58 and 62. *Don Thompson*

Deep into trolleybus territory Manor House was the furthest north point of the post war network. Car 2000 works Kingsway Subway service 33. The trip across London to West Norwood via 'The Tunnel' was timed at just over the hour. Conveniently situated around this intersection were pedestrian staircases that led to the tube station on the Piccadilly Line.

As service 33 made its way through inner North London, it negotiated this single track leading to Dove Road, formerly called Dorset Street. Although not unusual in London, one way working in separate streets was known to tram enthusiasts as 'canon hilling' after a particular fine specimen in Birmingham. *Don Thompson*

In the foreground tracks curve towards the northern portal of the Kingsway Subway. Before it descends into the depths car 1924 pauses at the loading island in Bloomsbury. A trolleybus on route 555 turns into Parton Street at the end of its journey from Leyton. *Don Thompson*

This is the single most important piece of tramway infrastructure to survive until the present day. Unfortunately it is now non operational. Car 1996 ascends the northern ramp to Southampton Row. Constructed by the London County Council in 1906 and enlarged for double deckers in 1931, the whole edifice had style. Note the ornate lamp standard over the mouth of the tunnel. *Don Thompson*

Holborn Tram Station is about to witness the departure of car 1964 northbound on service 31. It looks as if Don, the photographer, has the place to himself. Just to check on late arrivals, the driver pokes his head out. Passengers in the Subway entered and left via the driver's platform. *Don Thompson*

Not only passenger trams frequented the Subway. On 3rd April 1952 at 8.35 pm London Transport staff gather as snowbroom 037 is caught by the camera at Holborn Tram Station. Driven by Inspector G Harry Guilmartin this was the last single decker to pass through. The destination was the scrap yard at Penhall Road, Charlton.

High drama at the southern portal of the Subway. A crowd of spectators has gathered on Waterloo Bridge to observe the goings on beneath them. It appears the northbound track has been blocked. An LT inspector mans the points to give the right of way, wrong road working, to car 183 on service 31. The tram will use one of the two crossovers in the tunnel between here and Aldwych Station in order to regain the correct track. *Don Thompson*

Tracks along the Victoria Embankment were de facto reserved for trams; motor traffic steered clear of them. They formed a large terminal loop for many South London services. In this view the tramway sanctum has already been invaded by bus replacement vehicles. This was the cause of several accidents due to carelessness by bus drivers. *Don Thompson*

5 Landmarks, Junctions and Termini

In the early 1950s tourist landmarks such as Westminster Bridge and Big Ben dominated the scene. Here the trams were bit part players; however, away from the visitor trail, and unlikely to feature on any 'See Britain' brochures, were the workaday streets with complicated junctions with a mesh of rails in the roadway. And who could forget the distinctive clatter of individual tramcars, as they passed over points and crossings? Then there were the termini. Without fuss the big red and cream tramcars would reverse and resume their journeys in the opposite direction. All these aspects of tramway operation held a fascination for the dedicated enthusiast.

Tooley Street terminus in the shadow of London Bridge Station featured on film and in print. Car 840 stands in splendid isolation. On Sundays the busy world near the Pool of London was stilled with the neighboring warehouses and small shops closed and the service restricted to one tram every 12 minutes. The through journey to Greenwich was timed at just under half an hour. *Alan Watkins*

On the silver screen the end of the line for service 70 at Tooley Street, London Bridge was portrayed in the 1951 film *Pool of London*, which also featured a conversation in the upper saloon of a tram. Readers are directed towards this scene, where the two principal characters talk about the coming abandonment of the trams. Nighttime shots of Camberwell Green later in the film add to the ambiance. Ironically, the Camberwell location starred again with a full page picture in Harry Williams' book on South London, which hardly had a kind word to say about trams in the landscape.

The terminus on Southwark Bridge also got the cinematic treatment in the 1947 film *Hue & Cry*. Amongst the vehicles seen traversing the bridge are several Felthams. Published in 1951, Lucy Masterman's book *London from the Bus Top - A Guide for the Impecunious Traveller* acts as a guide to interesting sites. One suspects the volume appeared on the book shelves just in time for readers to savour the delights of the chapter on tram route 70, which linked London Bridge with Greenwich, before a bus bearing the same route number took over.

There were a number of very sharp bends on the system. As the tram 'bit' into the curve, the perspective for passengers changed quickly, sometimes too quickly for comfort. For children looking out of the top deck front windows, the screech of the wheels and swaying of the bodywork added to the fun! Here at the corner of Jamaica Road and Lower Road car 595 passes RT188 on route 47, which paralleled the trams along Jamaica Road as far as London Bridge. *Don Thompson*

The temporary lifting bridge spanning Deptford Creek also attracted the attention of tram enthusiasts. It was constructed to the well known Scherzer design. Again, London Transport was criticised in allocating funds for the supposed 'doomed' trams. This was another example of new conduit tracks being installed. They had a very short life. Car 585 is working service 70, which together with the 68 perished on 10th July 1951. *Alan Watkins*

Trams served the historic centre of Greenwich. Car 1873 is pictured here in Romney Road, which bisected the manicured lawns separating the Royal Naval College and the National Maritime Museum, overlooked by the world famous Royal Observatory. Lines of trees adjacent to ornamental railings lent an air of imperial, nautical style to the whole area. This scene remains basically the same today, although sadly without the trams. *Don Thompson*

The southern portal of the Blackwall Tunnel, opened by the London County Council in 1897, remains a local landmark. Here on an atmospheric, misty day by the Thames car 159 pauses at the end of the track before returning to Camberwell Green. The LCC once had plans to connect the northern and southern systems by a service of single deck trams through the tunnel.

Unusual rail layouts fascinated tramway students, especially when the conduit was included. There is scarcely room to spare at this single siding flanked by two through tracks in Blackfriars Road on the approach to the bridge. Such was the demand for tram rides from the London public on the last day (5th July 1952) that vehicles had to be shunted to augment the service.
John Gillham

The Woolwich street market at Beresford Square featured in London tramway folklore, the more so after the demise of the trams, because rails and points survived into the 1970s. It became a place of pilgrimage for industrial archaeologists. Car 312 waits on the terminal loop. Service 44 was basically the Eltham short working of service 46 which covered the same tracks. Note the smartly dressed shoppers.

In the last week of London's trams car 169 is depicted on the single track in Green's End, Woolwich, as it approaches the terminus at Beresford Square. This area has now changed, and not for the better. Sadly, where the Luftwaffe failed, town planners, property developers and highway engineers succeeded, rendering the centre of Woolwich a soulless concrete desert. The Royal Arsenal Gate directly in front of the tram did survive the carnage; it is now a listed building. *Don Thompson*

New Cross Station still displays its green Southern Railway sign, which rather overshadows the London Transport 'UNDERGROUND' roundel, alerting passengers to the presence of the East London line of the Metropolitan. Summer dresses and shirt sleeves attest to this warm July day in 1952. Car 1980 still looks good for many years service, as it traverses New Cross Road. Unfortunately, its career ended in Penhall Road scrap yard in October of the same year. Note the almost complete lack of motor traffic. *Don Thompson*

This service 12 tram at Nine Elms Lane forms part of a artistic study of overhead pipes and conveyor belts. Thameside wharves, factories and the old steam railway sheds for stabling locomotives serving Waterloo Station once occupied this area. All has now been swept away. *Alan Watkins*

The Peckham Rye terminus of routes 56/84 probably laid claim to be the quietest on the system. Situated in a suburban backwater, locals could reach central London from here in around half an hour, whereas the bus on circular route 173 remained close to base and only served Peckham. *Alan Watkins*

No book on the landscape of London's tramways would be complete without a mention of the four track Dog Kennel Hill, which was on the main tram route linking Camberwell Green with Catford. Safety rules required that on the ascent and descent no two trams could occupy the same track. Prior to tramway abandonment this was electric traction territory; no central buses tackled the gradient. *Don Thompson*

Gents outside the 'gents', who are consumed with reading the newspaper, form an historic cameo of London life. Not even the close approach of car 169 in St George's Road can catch their attention. It was said LCC highways engineers favoured public conveniences of this type, because rainwater collected in the conduit could then be flushed straight through the facility next door. *Don Thompson*

The folks who lived in this part of London were certainly spoilt for choice when it came to public transport. Trams, trolleybuses and motor buses competed for custom. The main line railway station at Clapham Junction was also just round the corner. Car 1768 on service 26 is about to reverse, to be followed by car 1841 on service 28 to Victoria. *Don Thompson*

This is how the Bricklayers Arms junction looked before mass demolition sacrificed the place to the motor car. With not a flyover in sight, car 1614 emerges from the northern end of Old Kent Road to cross tracks leading to Tower Bridge Road, used by service 68. *Don Thompson*

6 Riding the 16/18

Dr Gerald Druce, a mechanical engineer by profession, also had an abiding interest in tramways, especially those of his native Croydon. In October 2010 he sent the following reminiscences to your author. Included in the text are technical details of the trams and the routes they served, particularly the 16/18 service from Purley to the Embankment.

'...For the first few years of his life your correspondent lived in the extreme north of the (then) County Borough of Croydon, close to the boundary with the (then) London County Council.

Returning to Norbury after wartime evacuation your correspondent was quickly rewarded by a sight of the magnificent LCC car 1 in service; he witnessed the replacement in daylight of the scissors crossover on the Croydon side of the boundary by a trailing crossover. The scissors had been the terminus of Croydon service 1 (Norbury to Purley) before through running with the LCC began in 1926. The LCC cars on service 16/18 reversed on a trailing crossover on the opposite side of the boundary, through passengers

A column of traffic, including a 708 Green Line coach bound for East Grinstead, plus a threesome of buses, pauses for the lights on Brixton Hill. Leading the pack is Feltham car 2148. One would not expect a quick getaway on the green. Although modern and comfortable, type UCC trams were sluggish on gradients. *Don Thompson*

Car 2125 is pictured at Streatham change pit, where very shortly the conductor will haul down the trolley pole, in order to continue the journey on the conduit. According to Dr Druce, he witnessed many tram crews making short work of the transition from conduit to overhead wire. *Gerald Druce*

had to alight and walk the few feet to the waiting Croydon Corporation car. Such inconveniences, common at municipal boundaries, were 'gifts' to the rival bus operators. Within your correspondent's experience, the new crossover was always used, except on one occasion when cars arrived simultaneously on opposite sides of the new crossover and both were due to reverse!

Through running was to the obvious advantage of both operators, but involved more than filling in the 10 inch (25 cm) gap between the tracks. The LCC insisted on the use of top covered trams. The Croydon authorities began under the happy delusion that putting a top cover on their 1902 bogie trams solved that problem, these were the cars I encountered on the Thornton Heath branch. Put right, they ordered ten new trams in 1926 and another fifteen soon after. They closely resembled the LCC E/1 trams of the 1775-1851 series, but had transverse upholstered seats on both decks from new, reducing the top deck capacity from 46 to 42. The (65hp) motors and controllers came from a different manufacturer (GEC) to those who equipped LCC trams.

In London Transport days they could be distinguished from a genuine E/1 by the large stencil number indicators in each end top deck window and, to the knowledgeable, by the oval hole in the plough carrier. Being higher than the Croydon open toppers, it was necessary to lower the roadway under the railway bridge at Norbury to accommodate the new cars. Just enough space was allowed for the new cars, and their LCC counterparts, to squeeze cautiously through: as this section was liable to flood, the original level was restored when the tram tracks were lifted in the summer of 1952.

Tracks in the County Borough of Croydon were usually well maintained and gave a smooth ride in contrast to their conduit counterparts north of the Surrey border. The lorry driver closely pursuing car 1912 ought to be aware that the tram has very effective magnetic brakes. Slow speed collisions accounted for much of the accidental damage, as motor traffic increased in post war years. *Don Thompson*

To obtain adequate clearance, the overhead wire was offset from the track, pushing the pole as low as possible clear of the nearside of the car. One consequence was a slack trolley rope; once your correspondent saw it loop around the rear headlight, taking up the slack prevented the pole from rising as the wire resumed the normal height, so the current supply was lost on the rising gradient. The driver first assumed the circuit breaker had tripped, although he should have heard it as it was just above his head, but belatedly he applied the handbrake before the car ran back. Detective work to locate the problem followed!

Further work preparatory to through running involved relaying the track all the way from Norbury to Purley (5.75 miles, 8km) on a concrete foundation paved with asphalt. Not weakened by any conduit it proved long lasting, giving a reasonably smooth ride and good quality paving up to the end.

From 1945 to 1950 your correspondent travelled to school and then to his first job by tram, on ex Croydon track with overhead current collection all the way. These journeys involved service 16/18, giving the opportunity to observe cars on service 42. Occasional visits to London introduced him to the mysteries of the conduit and the Kingsway Subway. Hence, on mature reflection, your correspondent realises that his experience of the London tramways between 1945 and 1951 was atypical, both as regards the quality of the track and the types of tram he rode on.

Before the scrapping programme commenced, cars on 16/18 were provided by Telford Avenue and Thornton Heath Depots. Neither of their allocations followed the LCC principle of grouping cars fitted with the same make of controller and motors at one depot. Telford Avenue accommodated all the Felthams; the ex Metropolitan Electric and London United cars had different makes of controller and of motor; the experimental cars, 2165 and 2167, were different again. Although an ex LCC depot, the only ex LCC vehicle was the magnificent car 1. Thus every air braked car then on the system was at this depot.

The stock was completed with the notorious ex Walthamstow cars, which lived a peripatetic existence ever since London Transport took them away from their native home, so quickly that most were still in their original colours. Eighteen survived to 1945, the two differently equipped batches (2042 - 2053 and 2054 - 2061) further extended the variety of spare parts needed at Telford Avenue. In contrast Thornton Heath Depot continued to house the 23 ex Croydon Corporation cars (375 - 399 less 376 and 396) made up with ex LCC E/3 cars 1904 - 1918; the two types were used indiscriminately on services 16/18 and 42. The 42 was confined within the Croydon boundary and hence ran entirely on the overhead. Thus all the cars your correspondent rode on had comfortable seats, moreover about half the journeys he made were on air braked cars with heaters (lacking on contemporary LT motor buses), and most of his travels were on good track with overhead current collection.

The buildings on the right of the picture are a sure sign the motoring age has arrived with a vengeance. On Streatham High Road car 1941 approaches the open space of Streatham Common. It is passing the Pied Bull pub, still in business today, though regulars no longer have the privilege of arriving on the 16/18 tram. *Don Thompson*

These attributes almost certainly account for the reliability he experienced. His daily journey to work involved the last WORKMAN on service 16/18 from Norbury at 7.30 am to Croydon (running number 26). A Telford Avenue working, almost always a Feltham, it came through from the Embankment. The rear destination indicator was set to display WORKMAN (rarely photographed). He does not remember ever being late for work due to a tramway delay. Coming home he caught running numbers 11 or 13, both Thornton Heath workings, an E/3 or an ex Croydon bogie car, only experiencing one delay, which was due to the driver of a private car unwisely overtaking a tram on the offside only to collide head on with another tram coming in the opposite direction.

The outer section of 16/18 had the benefit of two directional rush hours, as it served commuters working in London and in Croydon. From 1947 to

At the corner of Parchmore Road and High Street, Thornton Heath, the Clock Tower stands opposite the local branch of Woolworth's. Croydon route 42 was a survivor of the municipal tramway era, when elected officials were enthusiastic in installing the latest public transport the Edwardian age had to offer. In the corporate climate of London Transport it was very lucky to survive as long as it did. *Don Thompson*

1950 the workman's fare from Norbury Station to Crown Hill, Croydon (3 miles) was 4d (1.67p) return, cars ran every 4 minutes. The ordinary fare was 4d single, off peak the 3d cheap midday fare was available between 10.00 am and 4.00 pm Mondays to Fridays.

The Croydon area had its own quota of transfer fares: at Thornton Heath Pond between the branch and the main line in both directions and, preserving the ex Croydon portions of the abandoned routes to Norwood and Addiscombe, at designated points in the town centre. A consequence was the need to print special tickets for all denominations involved, including those for the trolleybus and motor bus services on the replacement routes. The transfer facilities disappeared abruptly with the 1950 fare increase with the consequence that the 2½d transfer from Norbury Station to Thornton Heath High Street became 3d+2d=5d, an increase of 100%...'

Brigstock Road, Thornton Heath is the setting for car 384 as it approaches a length of interlaced or gauntlet track. Usually employed as a substitute for single line, the one advantage was the lack of expenditure on points! Note the varied shops. The one with the famous SPRATTS dog biscuit sign also sells Brooke Bond Dividend Tea. Very popular in the 1950s, each packet contained a savings stamp. You collected 60 to exchange for five shillings (25p) worth of groceries. *Don Thompson*

Services 16/18 lasted long enough to traverse the new Festival of Britain gyratory layout. Here Feltham car 2140 edges gingerly round one of the newly laid curves. Tram drivers appreciated having the roped off road area to themselves. *Don Thompson*

Purley terminus in the County of Surrey was the furthest point south of the capital reached by trams. Heading in the same direction, until late 1939, the next trams encountered would have been Brighton Corporation open toppers. In this thriving local shopping centre Feltham car 2153 is about to reverse for the trek back to central London. Somehow the replacing bus route 109 will not be as exciting! *Don Thompson*

7 The Man on the Clapham Tram

The 'man' in this case was author and student of all things tramway, Julian Thompson. The phrase 'The Man on the Clapham Omnibus' is attributed to Lord Bowen and aims to describe a professional member of the middle class and how he would approach a legal problem in a common sense way. Of course, 'the Workman on the Clapham Tramcar' would not have qualified, when the original phrase was coined! Such was the class ridden state of the nation.

Julian attempted to remedy something of the situation and your author acknowledges Julian's own suggestion for the title of this chapter. In an extensive correspondence Julian committed his memories to paper.

Cheers For Last Tram From Wimbledon

CROWD FORM GUARD AT CIVIC FAREWELL

Police Patrol New Bus Terminus Route

"Where's the gee-gees?" shouted a wag as the last tram on the service to Wimbledon pulled in to the terminus outside the Town Hall shortly before midnight on Saturday.

Hundreds of people turned out in a keen damp wind to see the tram which was to close the electrified service to the Embankment leave on its historic journey at 11.39 p.m. There were people in evening dress, homegoing workers, Saturday night dancers, and those who wanted to recall proudly as the years go by that they saw the last tram leave Wimbledon. There seemed to be some doubt as to which was the last tram, and a number of people boarded the next to last, probably thinking that they were helping to make history.

TRAM No. 1847

As the last tram came in, the crowd on either side of the track formed a guard of honour. It came to its last halt at the Wimbledon terminus, and Press photographers with flash apparatus formed up in the road. The Mayor of Wimbledon (Coun. J. E. C. Stroud), with chain of office, left the Town Hall and walked over to the terminus, accompanied by Ald. Cyril W. Black, M.P., Ald. and Mrs. W. E. Hamlin, and Coun. J. E. V. Campbell. The Mayor noticed that the tram was No. 1847. He asked with a smile if 1847 was the year when the service started. A tram-man gave him an old-fashioned look. As Wimbledon's public figures bade farewell to the tram and its crew there was a succession of camera flashes.

Then there was a surge forward as people clambered aboard. "Let's have three halfpennyworth," said a youth to his pal, but by the time they had walked a few steps the tram had filled up, gangways as well.

A cheer went up as the driver started the tram on its last journey, and someone showered streamers on the crowd from the tram's platform.

It turned round the bend and went out of sight. Before its last "clankety-clank" had become inaudible the tram terminus was almost deserted. Another page in the book of time had turned over, and only a memory remained.

The bus services which replace the trams have a terminus in St. George's-road and Francis-grove. St. George's-road usually flanked

with parked vehicles, was kept clear this week by a police patrol. There has been a change in the buses serving Plough-lane, Haydons-road and South Wimbledon area. The No. 189 North Cheam to Cannon-street Station, has replaced route 5a. On Saturdays and Sundays route 189a will operate between Raynes Park and Clapham Common, replacing route 5, with an extension to Cannon-street Station up till midday on Saturday.

FAREWELL TO 9 TRAM ROUTES

120 NEW BUSES WILL TAKE OVER

"Evening News" Industrial Correspondent

SIXTY-THREE miles of London tram routes will disappear this weekend, London Transport announce to-day.

Nearly 120 latest-type buses are being marshalled on a special site in Edgware for the take-over and will cross London in convoy on Saturday afternoon.

Tram routes which go out at Saturday midnight are 2, 4, 6, 8, 10, 20, 22 and 24, and all-night 1.

The change over means the end of trams in Wimbledon, Merton, Colliers Wood, Tooting, Balham and Clapham, and their partial disappearance in Wandsworth, Lambeth, Southwark, the City, and Westminster, including four Embankment routes.

The Details

The last tram in the area will be the 12.21 a.m. Sunday morning Tooting-Brixton, driven by 35-year-old Robert Miles, of Jessop-road, Herne Hill, with 24-year-old Kenneth Frost, of Tunstall-road, Brixton, conductor.

Here are details of the new bus routes: 155, Wimbledon Station-Embankment (via Westminster), replacing tram route 2; 155b, Wimbledon Station-Embankment (via Blackfriars), replacing tram route 4; 189, North Cheam-Cannon-street Station, replacing tram route 5 and bus route 5a (at City and terminus will be Dowgate-hill); 95, Tooting-broadway-Cannon-street, Station (via Streatham and Brixton), replacing tram route 10; 57a, Streatham (St. Leonard's Church)-Victoria (via Tooting and Clapham), replacing tram route 8; 57, Tooting-broadway-Victoria (via Streatham and Brixton), replacing tram route 20; 104, Tooting (Mitre)-Embankment (Horse Guards-avenue) (via Clapham and Vauxhall), replacing tram route 22 in weekday peaks only; 30, Streatham (Telford-avenue) (via Brixton and Vauxhall), replacing tram route 24 in weekday peaks only; 28 (all-night route), Tooting circular, replacing tram route 1.

The Mayor of Wimbledon (Coun. J. E. C. Stroud) shakes hands with the driver of the last tram from Wimbledon just before it left the terminus on Saturday night.

In the summer of 1907 the first tramcar leaving Worple-road was given a civic send-off in the presence of hundreds of Wimbledon residents.

59

'....In very early days of my touring, about 1947, I discovered route 58. My ride from the Oval went on and on, I was fascinated by the right angled curves at Forest Hill. Shortly after, the conductor came up to the top deck, and enquired how far I thought I could go for 4d! From our house in Hillbury Road S.W.17 it was possible to hear trams in Balham High Road, when they were stopping at and starting from the stop at Ritherdon Road.

The Westminster Regulator, by name of Drury, was pleased to receive a copy of my skit 'Tramway Follies', based loosely on the Gilbert and Sullivan operas. This was in the 1950 period, when many officials were quite pro tram, but could not state so in public. There is a press record of a staff member claiming that trams were the finest form of transport ever invented; I don't know what LT thought of this.

Another unusual thing was the method of changing crews at New Cross. Many of the waiting crews sat on a low wall in New Cross Road at the junction with Pepys Road. Crews who were late caused serious delays to services, and it was common to see a line of London bound trams held up, and stretching back to New Cross Station.

On a damp, dismal night at Wimbledon, both these trams present a welcome sight for passengers wanting to get out of the rain. The car on the right is probably on a depot working as far as Clapham, whilst sister vehicle 1810 is going the whole way to the Victoria Embankment. At times like this the top deck windows would steam up in response to the actions of cigarette and pipe smokers on board. *Don Thompson*

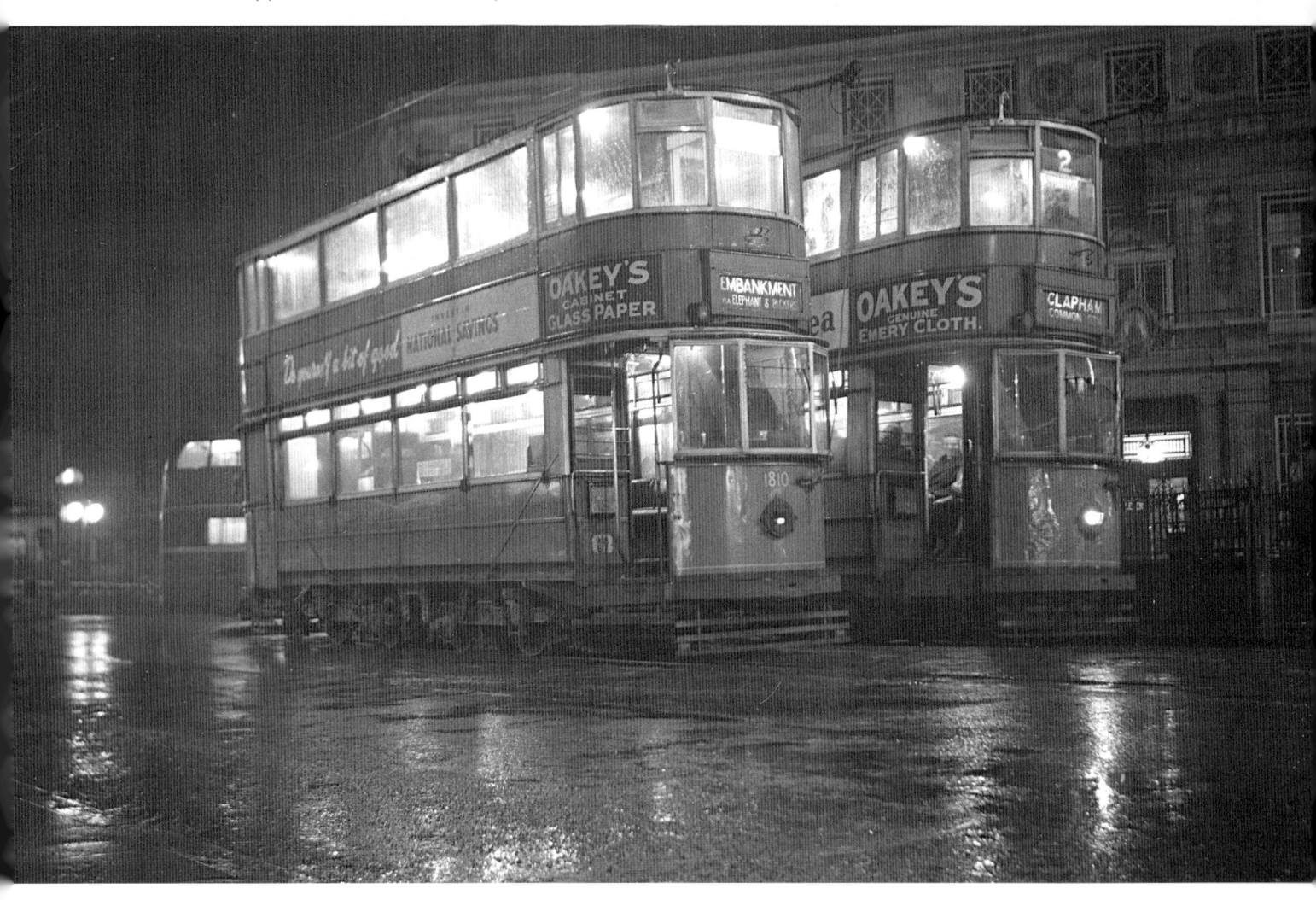

Car 1841 surmounts the hump back bridge over the River Wandle on its way north to central London. Note the neat overhead wiring. This section had once formed part of the London United Electric Tramways empire, the brainchild of Sir James Clifton Robinson. The rails from Wimbledon terminus to Tooting came under LCC control in 1922. *Don Thompson*

The press cuttings include many human interest stories, and some unusual facets of tramway operation. I qualify more than most people to represent 'the man on the Clapham tram' because of a funny incident. On one occasion I did not hear the conductor of a northbound car call out "All Change" when it stopped in Clapham High Street, outside the depot. Suddenly the car reversed into the shed, with me on the top deck.

As you know, I wrote down my experiences in my *London Trams in Camera* book, published in 1971. Since you may not have a copy (it is now out of print), I shall endeavour to enlighten you. As regards the 'man on the Clapham tram' experience it is worth repeating my notes taken at the time on a spring day in 1949.

The through service between the Embankment and Wimbledon Hill commenced in 1922. From 1926 until 1931, when the London United section closed, services 2/4 were extended at weekends to Hampton Court. Unfortunately that impressive ride was before my time. When the LUT trolleybuses arrived, the tram terminus was cut back to Wimbledon Town Hall, where it remained for the rest of the tramway era.

The car I took for this journey was 1787 of class E/1, newly repainted and allocated to Clapham Depot. It was the first car I had seen with lower deck bracing straps, which were an LT attempt to keep body and soul together, before the vehicle was eventually sent to its fiery end at Penhall Road. I paid 11d for a return ticket to Wimbledon. Another top deck passenger had

When the carriageway narrowed, double track gave way to single line. Here on Merton Road S.W.19. we are a few stops away from Wimbledon terminus. Car 1809 was one of the Clapham Depot stalwarts. Don told me he thought the two cyclists rather spoilt the picture, but the reader may disagree, as we view this summer scene in the suburbs taken around 1950. *Don Thompson*

a 5d workman return for the 13 mile round trip from Balham Station to the Embankment - great value for money. After some slow running between County Hall and Kennington, we were further slowed by large crowd of potential passengers at The Oval. The tram in front was already full and the conductor prevented anyone else boarding his car.

We then quickened the pace. With a full load on board 1787 performed well, up to and slightly beyond the 30 mph speed limit. Passing the loading island at Stockwell tube station, we ran steadily along Clapham Road, under the South London Line railway bridge and reached the 'hole in the wall' entrance to Clapham Depot. As you know, this ex LCC shed was full of 'standards' - E/1 cars including mostly of the 1800 series.

The Plough, Clapham was the limit of the 4d fare from central London. It was also where service 34 branched off right to go along the north side of the common. I used to enjoy looking out over Clapham Common on this stretch before Clapham South tube station. The landscape beyond became more depressing, as we encountered Balham and Tooting. At the Broadway the track layout was quite interesting, especially for drivers on service 20 who had to navigate round the south side of a statue of King Edward VII.

Trolleybus overhead wires used by routes 630 and 612 crossed here, although since we were on the conduit, there were no overhead crossings between the two forms of electric traction, as existed on London Road, West Croydon at the junction with Tamworth Road.

Onward down the gentle slope to Longley Road change pit. Here we switched current collection, the conductor raised the pole and more people got on the car. We crossed the River Wandle and passed in front of Merton Bus Garage, one of the largest in London. There was single track and one loop in Merton Road. Normally the signals worked in our favour; there was no hold up. We then reached the terminus outside Wimbledon Town Hall. The track layout here featured a scissors crossover. As we entered, another car left on service 4 to the Embankment.

I could say a lot more about the return journey, but I'll leave it for now. Suffice to say tram services 2/4 perished on the night of 6th/7th January 1951, to be replaced by bus 155.'

The Longley Road change pit in Tooting was the location of the changeover from conduit to overhead trolley. The change pit attendant is about to fork the plough under car 1561. Meanwhile car 1562 moves forward in order to 'shoot' its plough from the carrier on the side of the tram. Note the row of conduit ploughs already stored to the left of the attendant.
Don Thompson

BISTO
For all
MEAT DISHES
10
via BRIXTON
KAVANAGH
1357

HAIRDRESSERS
34
WATNEY'S ALES
via CLAPHAM
ARTISTIC FLORIST
LOYDS BANK LIMITE
1377

Pictured under a web of trolleybus wires, car 1357 rumbles along Mitcham Road just round the corner from Tooting Broadway tram junction. The wires leading off to the right form part of Longmead Road turning loop. Note the lad on the top deck as he attempts to open one of the sliding windows. One advantage of these E/1 class rehab trams was the absence of a large route number stencil which partly obscured the view forward. For the record, car 1357 was scrapped in February 1951. *John Meredith*

In the centre of Clapham passenger safety islands ensured the well being of those waiting for trams. Car 1377, depicted here on service 34, is about to turn to the motorman's right in order to transverse Long Road and then Clapham Common North Side. Tracks straight ahead lead to Balham and Tooting. *John Meredith*

The junction of Clapham Road with Stockwell Road once boasted 144 trams an hour in peak times. In spite of this impressive figure, as can be seen here, there was no provision for passenger loading islands. Those who have just alighted from car 1836 take their lives in their hands, as they attempt to reach the side of the road. One could say this was tantamount to criminal neglect by London Transport. *Don Thompson*

Appendix A
Julian Thompson's Tramway Diary 1949-51

Many British tramways in their declining years fell victim to neglect. It was more expedient for management to find any excuse not to allocate funds for track and fleet maintenance. As the diary shows, this was not the case in London, where renewal of rails and infrastructure continued in the run up to abandonment.

17.1.49
A stretch of the westbound track just east of Charing Cross has recently been relaid. Half of it (the easternmost half) has been paved, but the rest is completely excavated, and I believe new conduit sections are being put in. The midday Evening Standard carries an explanation of the shortage of labour for maintaining London's tram tracks. Men regard it as a "dead-end" job, and while older men gradually retire, younger men are unwilling to take up this skilled work as the trams are likely to be scrapped in four or five years. Work is also being done on the up track just north of Lambeth Church. Today I saw these cars freshly out of Charlton:- 191, 388, 2160.

19.1.49
The down curve at the junction of Old Gloucester Street and Theobalds Road received attention yesterday. Today, the second crossover (going north) had the surrounding setts relaid. Down track just north of Lambeth Church is being relaid. During this afternoon a no 74 tram broke down on Blackfriars Bridge.

27.1.49
Track alongside loading island opposite Charing Cross tube stn. has recently been relaid.

28.1.49
Have recently seen cars 156 (HR/2) and 177 (E/3) freshly out of Charlton. A deep hole several feet in length has been dug below the s.bound track in Balham High Rd, opposite the site of the old depot. The conduit has been disconnected for several feet, and trams have to coast over the gap.

31.1.49
A no 72 tram broke down at Lambeth Baths at about 8.30a.m. today. A 30 min hold-up was caused.

1.2.49
Tramcar caught fire in Streatham High Road. Electrical equipment in driver's cab was responsible, I believe.

10.2.49
Trackwork is being repaired west of Waterloo Bdge. (both tracks), and east of it (eastbound track). Joints are being tightened. There was a hold up caused by a Feltham on the southbound curve at Blackfriars, at about 5.20p.m. today. Its lights were still on. It had a dent in its side, but I don't know if this had any connection with the business. Saw 1744 freshly out of Charlton. Two no 68 trams were fired at within an hour in Evelyn St, Deptford, on Monday. On Tuesday, another tram had its window holed near Tower Bridge.

17.2.49
Saw no: 164 (E/3) working on route 40. It is the only E/3 car at New Cross. A stretch of the eastbound track, immediately east of the Savoy St crossover, had recently been relaid.

20.2.49
Cars 115, 127, 399 and 1480 have recently been in Charlton. Some time ago a new tram stop sign, like those erected at bus stops, but blue was installed at the s. bound Westminster stop. Similar signs have lately been erected in High St South, Greenwich (s. bound track - Greenwich Church end), and in Upper Tooting Road (last up stop before Trinity Road tube station). The track alongside the loading island at Brixton Town Hall (down), has been relaid. None too soon, as it was worn very badly, cars running on their flanges for several yards.

24.2.49
Track is being relaid on the westbound, at Savoy St, immediately west of the crossover. Recently saw 1419 out of Charlton. Part of the up track just north of the crossover at the junc. of Kennington Rd. and Kennington Lane has been relaid.

4.3.49
The London Transport Executive today made a statement about the scrapping of the London trams. They are to be scrapped in nine stages, starting in the west, and working across London to Charlton. Replacement by buses is expected to start in 1950, and will take about three years. Thornton Heath, Clapham, Telford Ave, Camberwell, New Cross, Wandsworth, and Abbey Wood depots will become bus garages. The outer curve at Blackfriars has been relaid, but the track is still "open".

11.3.49
Yesterday saw no: 1444 (ME/3) and 385 (CCT) freshly out of Charlton. Today saw 2121 (UCC) and 1766 (E/1). The outer curve at Blackfriars: now completely finished. A stretch of the up track opposite the Granada Cinema, Kennington, has recently been relaid. Some track joints between the Oval and Stockwell were being tightened today.

12.3.49

On the 27th February work was proceeding on the Harders Rd reverser (Apparently part of the reverser has been removed, and the down track reinstated. (SEE DRAWING). The up track at Clapham South, between the crossings giving access to the turning circle, has recently been relaid.

13.3.49

The crossing of the turning circle across the up track, at Clapham South, has been removed, and the points fossilised. The crossing was removed yesterday, after the track had been "open" for a few days (SEE DRAWING). This is the second reverser that has been curtailed in the last three weeks. The down just north of Rushey Green is being relaid The action of the L.T.E. in removing parts of the reversers seems quite pointless. They cannot now be used for reversing cars, and can only be used for storing them.

26.3.49

All the points and crossings have now been removed from the turning circle at Clapham South (SEE DRAWING AT END OF APPENDIX) - the conduit "points"only remain. Car no 1787 has recently appeared from Charlton with diagonal bracing struts, (like 1779) from window sills at ends of saloon to bogie centre. A new blue stop sign has been installed at New Cross Gate. The following cars have recently appeared out of Charlton:- 93, 389, 594, 1251, 1770, 1798.

30.3.49

At midnight last night a water main burst in Newington Butts (just s. of the Elephant & Castle), flooding the tramway to a depth of one foot. All night services were diverted via Walworth Road. By 9a.m. today, cars were operating UP only and all today only trams were allowed in the affected section of road, between the Elephant and Draper St. (up which street northbound motor-traffic was diverted). Cars were operating normally in the evening. Saw 1787 with the new-fangled bracing. Cars so equipped are 1779, 1798, 1787. One of the new blue stop signs has been placed in position at New Cross Gate. On 26th March car 159 bound for Clapham and points north collided with a petrol tanker on the north side of Battersea Bridge. The front of the car was badly burned. The lorry driver was seriously injured.

10.4.49

The practice of installing the new blue stop signs is now fairly general. They are exactly like bus stops but merely say "Tram Stop", with no distinction between compulsory and request stops. All the large signs which formerly hung at the principal stop on the 2/4 route (giving the places served by northbound trams) have now been removed. I have recently noticed 117, 1038, 1175, 1532, 1654 and 1743 freshly out of Charlton.

25.4.49

Have recently seen these cars freshly out of Charlton:- 88, 380, 1602, 1761, 1958, 2094. Last week there were several tramway mishaps.

1.5.49

I have recently seen the following cars newly out of Charlton:- 143, 375, 1896, 2087, 2140. Track-laying is taking place at the following points: 1. near Surrey Docks (up road); 2. Just south of Bricklayer's Arms (down road). Track has also been recently relaid just north of Balham Station (down road). 1809 has appeared with external bracing, as the other cars, but has not been repainted. 1597 has been repaired, it is reported.

6.5.49

Have recently noticed these cars out of Charlton:- 1096, 1495, 1549, 1958. About a week ago work commenced on tightening the track joints in Kennington Rd, at the Lambeth Road end. The up track was attended to. A day or so ago work was commenced on the down (and worst) track. Oxy-acetylene apparatus is being used.

19.5.49

Work continues on Kennington Road. The joints on the down track have been attended to, and now the men are working towards the Horns Tavern. Have recently noticed the following cars out of Charlton:- 179, 383, 1553, 1743, 1781 (with external bracing), 1950, 2085, 2124. Track has recently been relaid on the down opposite Balham Hippodrome, and on both up and down tracks at the bottom of Green Lanes, Streatham.

23.5.49

Track is being attended to just north of the Norbury Hotel - on the down road. Work continues on Kennington Rd. 1786 has appeared with external bracing - but has not been in Charlton (overhauled). Noticed an ordinary E/1 operating on route 12. The E/1s at Wandsworth are usually confined to the 26s.

25.5.49

A no 22 crashed into a no 16 outside Lambeth Town Hall today. Noticed 397, 88, 1350 freshly out of Charlton.

5.6.49

The following cars have recently been repainted:- 93, 337, 1223, 1225, 574, 1565, 1363, 1762, 1887, 1553, 1773 (also been fitted with external bracing), and 1802 similarly fitted. Much track laying has been done of recent weeks in the Woolwich Road near Charlton. Track is being relaid on the up road just east of the Elephant & Castle. 1824 has been fitted with external bracing without being overhauled. A bad track joint opposite the loading island at Savoy St. has been attended to.

14.6.49

Relaying is in progress on the inside curve at Blackfriars. This work began yesterday. Have recently seen cars 2, 1493, 1961, 2154, which have been overhauled. 1818 has had external bracing fitted but has not been repainted. The down track in Kennington Rd is becoming very bad. The up track is in poor condition, north of Fitzalan St, but does not impart a pitching motion to the cars as it did before it was attended.

25.6.49

There has been much relaying of both up and down tracks in the New Kent Rd, and also less extensive renewals in the Old Kent Rd. Part of the up track, just south of the Plough junction has received six new rails. Work proceeds on the inside curve at Blackfriars. About a week ago work was begun to extend the Westminster loading island southwards, as shewn in drawing (SEE DRAWING). Exchange tickets were in use 13.6. - 25.6. inclusive. They were given in exchange for transfer tickets, on the second journey. The object of this believed to be to check on little used transfers, and abolish them. The following cars have recently been overhauled,- 340, 342, 1208, 1390, 1763, 1803 (with external bracing), 2154, 2159.

10.7.49

The following cars have recently appeared repainted - 1007, 1140, 1595, 1758, 1855, 1857, 1984, 2161, 312. Ex-Croydon car 387 has appeared with external bracing, and is the only car of this type so fitted, I believe. Track relaying is proceeding in Croydon High St, almost opposite the junction with Mint Walk (down track); also on the Embankment, on the outer track just before the facing crossover at Blackfriars.

2.7.49

Work will very soon be complete on the new rolling lift bridge at Deptford Creek. The drawing shows the situation up to 17th July: cars travel DOWN via the old bridge, and UP via the new (SEE DRAWING). These cars have recently been overhauled:- 344, 580, 1778 (with external bracing, 1893, 1962; 387 has external bracing, possibly the only CCT so treated. Saw a Feltham on route 24 today. It is the first time I have ever seen one on either route 22 or 24.

1.8.49

Have recently noticed the following cars repainted and overhauled:- 559, 560, 562, 302, 1597, 1806, 1809 - last two with external bracing. Today a route 8 car in the Balham High Rd. caught fire, and was taken to Clapham Depot.

10.8.49

The following cars have recently been overhauled and repainted:- 302, 304, 1769, 1860, 1998. There were two tram hold-ups on 8th August. A tram broke a plough at Lambeth Town Hall, causing 12 minutes' delay. A no: 72 broke down in Westminster Bridge Rd. A new loading island came into use at Victoria on 3rd August (SEE DRAWING).

20.8.49

The following cars have recently been repainted etc:- 802, 565, 1216, 1252, 1793, 1884; 1791 has not been repainted but has external bracing, A section of the down part of the Horns junction has been renewed. There were many loose joints on the down in Clapham Rd, between Stockwell and Lansdowne Way. They have received some attention, but are still bad.

31.8.49

The following cars have recently been overhauled, etc:- 135, 309, 1369, 1758, 1769, 1832, 1891, 2097, 2098. 1835 has external bracing, but has apparently not been overhauled etc. Track relaying is taking place at the following points: opposite entrance to Temple Stn, (both roads); up track in South Lambeth Rd, just s. of junction with Wilcox Rd; up track at junction of Lee Rd and Lee High St, now completed. The sections of track with loose joints (1) down between Lansdowne Way and Swan Stockwell (2/4); down between Clapham North Stn and Clapham Manor St. have now been attended to and are slightly improved.

13.9.49

Cars recently overhauled are:- 103, 307, 575, 1555, 1771, 1775, 1895, 1959, 2001. Track in South Lambeth Rd is being relaid - (1) Just s. of junction with Fentiman Rd. (2) just s. of Aldebert Terr. (3) between Swan and Lansdowne Way - all on UP track. Paving is being relaid on e. bound midway between Savoy St. and Charing Cross.

9.10.49

The track at Lewisham Clock Tower junction has recently been renewed. Much relaying is also taking place at various points between Forest Hill and Goose Green. The following cars have recently been repainted and overhauled:- 158, 195, 166, 308, 1850, 1861, 1960, 2003, ~101, 2107, 2142. The stock number appearing on the side panel, just above the rear bogie, is in white on recently done cars. Hitherto it has been in black.

10.11.49

The following cars have recently been repainted etc:- 153, 1088, 1174, 1567, 1660, 1848, 1951, 2054. The down track opposite Lassell St, Greenwich, is being relaid. A crossing at the junction of Southwark St. and Blackfriars Rd. has recently been renewed (SEE DRAWING). Beginning on the 19th October, the normal service on routes 2/4 has been cut from 30 to 24 cars per hour. This means that the service up to Kennington is now 5 minutes, and via Westminster or Blackfriars 10 minutes, as against 4 and 8 minutes before. However I have observed extras on route 4 operating to Blackfriars only (evening peak); they bear the running numbers 25, 26, 27, 28. Route 6 has been cut back to Tooting Broadway since 19th October.

23.11.49

Cars recently repainted etc, include:- 116, 128, 136, 137, 156, 2102, 2103, 2104, 1799. The points below have been relaid:- Greenwich Church (facing); Lewisham Clock Tower (facing); Rushey Green (trailing on west side of junction); Forest Hill (facing and crossing). Joints on the down track in Kennington Rd. between Fitzalan St and Kennington Lane seen to.

18.12.49
There has been much relaying in Kennington Road in the last two or three weeks. DOWN TRACK (1) from Lambeth Baths to half way between Brook Drive and Walcott Sq; (2) Curve and straight section up to the Horns; (3) At and approaching stop at junction with Kennington Lane. UP TRACK (1) From Brook Drive to half way between that point and Walcot Sq.; (2) Opposite Granada Cinema. Relaying has also been carried out on both tracks north of the Horns. I have not seen 2167 for a long time now. Work is reported to have started on converting Telford Ave. depot to take motor-buses.

19.1.50
Track has recently been renewed on the down road between the Horns and the junction of the Brixton & Clapham roads. These cars have recently been repainted etc.- 310, 301, 390 (with external bracing), 142, 203, 183, 1042, 1830, 1913, 2135. One of the ME/3 cars was lately been damaged in an accident - 1103. Work is well advanced on the scrap yard at Charlton. On 1st January, at midnight, all the cars at Thornton Heath moved to Purley Depot. Also in the new year work was begun on demolishing the Southern shed at Telford Ave. At present this shed is roofless, and the walls are partly missing. However the southern roads in the shed are still in use. Apparently Felthams 2165 and 2167 have been scrapped. I have certainly not seen the latter for some months.

12.2.50
The following cars have recently been overhauled, etc.:- 113, 126, 142, 961, 1366, 1538, 1492, 1783, 1814, 1826, 1830, 1873. 961 has appeared with external bracing, and is the first of the earlier series E/1s to be so treated. Several parts of the junction at Stockwell have been renewed. The trailing points connecting the Penhall Rd scrap yard with the Woolwich Rd have been paved, though entrance curve is incomplete. A change-pit is being constructed immediately inside the entrance, and poles for the overhead wires have been erected in the main road. Due to a road subsidence, the crossover at the junction of Stanstead Rd. and Brockley Rise is being relaid. The work has taken a week so far, and it will be another three weeks before it is completed.

10.3.50
The following cars have recently been repainted:- 201, 298, 384, 1609, 1784, 1827, 1884, 1923, 2132, 2144, 2150, 2162. The up road opposite the High St entrance of Clapham Depot has been relaid. Several joints on the down, just south of the railway bridge have been tightened, but there are many loose ones still. The roundabout for the County Hall was begun several weeks ago. (SEE DRAWING).

14.4.50
Joints are being tightened on the down s. of The Cut (Blackfriars Rd.) Much of the eastbound track between Charing Cross and Savoy St. has been relaid. Following cars have been repainted:- 399, 595, 1316, 1784, 1795, 1797, 1815,

1826, 1827, 1833, 1847, 2102, 2076, 2129, 2144. Standards at Penhall Rd. are in position, though only span wires in the yard itself have so far been erected. Thornton Heath depot is now completely demolished. The south shed at Telford Ave is roofless, but the two southernmost roads (on an inclined ramp) are still used for storing cars.

8.5.50
Cars 332 , 982, 601, 1005, 1562, 1801, 1907, 1932, 2092 have recently been repainted. Track relaying has been taking place in Loampit Vale (both tracks) immediately north of the Obelisk. The down road has recently received new rails also, between Lewisham Clock Tower and the Obelisk. The up track has been relaid south of the three-track layout in Blackfriars Rd. For progress on the County Hall roundabout - SEE DRAWING.

11.6.50
The north side of the County Hall roundabout was opened to trams and other traffic this morning (SEE DRAWING). The following cars have recently been repainted:- 171, 207, 138; 588, 589, 593, 1566, 1798, 1843, 1894, 2068, 2156, 2164.

12.7.50
The north side of the County Hall roundabout is now completely paved. The points at the junction of Westminster Bridge Rd and York Rd have been fossilised for the time being. The track between Stangate and Lambeth Palace Rd, forming part of the south side of the County Hall roundabout, has now been concreted up to bottom of rail level. The layout in the County Hall area is now as follows:(SEE DRAWING). There has been much relaying recently in Peckham Rd. The following cars have been in Charlton:- 295, 1226, 1570, 1507, 1787, 1909, 1897, 1947, 2119, 2141. The only remaining L.U.T. stop sign - at Stanley Rd, Wimbledon (n.bound) was removed about a fortnight ago.

16.7.50
Between 6a.m. on 14th July and 7a.m. this morning the section of Embankment between Horse Guards Parade and just east of Charing Cross Station was closed to traffic, while the Bailey Bridge was being completed. Cars northbound via Blackfriars Bridge mainly turned at Savoy St, but a few continued on to Charing Cross, returning on the wrong road, crossing over to the right one at Savoy St. Subway cars worked thus:- 33 via Kennington Rd, Lambeth Rd and Blackfriars Rd; 35 via London Rd and Blackfriars Rd. On Saturday and early today the 31s worked via Lambeth Rd. and Blackfriars Rd, but on Sunday worked normally to Westminster. Cars entered the Subway on the wrong road, crossing over to the correct one inside the Subway. Cars leaving the Subway first used the crossover inside the entrance to get onto the wrong track, then left the Subway on it. These operations of course meant that the points outside the Subway were used in the trailing direction instead of facing, and vice versa. A 2-car shuttle service was operated between Horse Guards Parade and Westminster (east crossover). The cars were 2058 and 2060, and had large notices EMERGENCY SHUTTLE SERVICE

pasted across three windows on each side. One car used the up track, the other the down. Lambeth Palace Rd is being excavated ready for the laying of tram track. The track which jutted out from the island into Stangate is now paved over, and surprisingly the pavement reinstated OVER the track!

17.8.50
Relaying has been taking place recently at the following points: Academy Rd. (both tracks); Stockwell Road (both tracks; some new conduit work on facing points at the North end of Parry St. Following cars have recently been into Charlton:- 174, 184, 1275, 1508, 157, 1657, 1671, 1781, 1787, 1794, 1805, 1841, 1848, 2079. The southern half of the County Hall roundabout now appears as follows (SEE DRAWING).

8.9.50
Sections of both tracks have recently been relaid between Rushey Green junction and Catford Stn. railway bridge. Track joints have been attended to on the down just north of Union Rd, Clapham. This was formerly a very bad section. Much progress has been made on the southern half of the County Hall roundabout, which now appears as follows (SEE DRAWING). The following cars have been observed repainted:- 170, 189, 1777, 1836, 2043, 2045, 2046, 2047, 1945, 2052, 2053.

24.8.50
A route 34 car ran away down Cedars Rd in the early morning of 23rd August, wrecking Hemming's shop on the NW corner of the junction. Only 3 people were injured. The upper deck of the tram (believed to be 1396) took the force of the crash. Cars 1383, 1385, 1654, and 1762, also 020, have been noted at Penhall Rd.

9.10.50
As cars due for scrapping left service on Sept. 30, they were run to Penhall Road. The next morning there were 58 new cars in the yard, also 20 Felthams being stored awaiting transport to Leeds. Tram routes 12, 26, 28, 31, 34 were replaced on October 1st by bus routes 44, 168, 169, 170 and 45 respectively. The 612 trolleybus route was also abandoned, and worked by the 12 tram replacement, this being a service from London Bridge to Mitcham Fair Green. 168 is extended to Wandsworth High St; 169 is unaltered. 170 leaves the former 31 route at Rosebery Ave. and extends to Well St. Hackney. 34 is extended to Farringdon St, and will be extended to South Kensington Stn. when Battersea Bridge is reopened. 168 uses the westbound tram track on Embanment when proceeding to Wandsworth. 170 uses this track from Savoy St to Westminster. Much of both tracks has been relaid between Horniman Museum and Forest Hill Stn. The up in Champion Park, and the up curve into Denmark Hill has also been relaid. The bad section between Clapham North Stn. and Manor St (down) has had the joints tightened. Cars 178, 187, 1675, 1824, 1968, 2048 have been repainted.

26.11.50
The southern half of the County Hall roundabout was opened on 22nd October. Much of both tracks between East Dulwich Stn and Forest Hill has been renewed in recent weeks. The western entrance curve to New Cross depot, also the trailing points, and parallel points in the depot yard have been relaid. In November six cars were damaged in a fire at Brixton Hill depot. 2162 and 2164 were seriously affected. For situation on opening day at County Hall (SEE DRAWING).

28.1.51
The following cars have been repainted in recent weeks:- 145, 180, 384, 394, 598, 1594, 1604, 1676, 1782, 1785, 1796, 1813, 1837, 1871, 1928, 1975, 1980, 2060. The up connecting curve at Lambeth Baths junction has been disconnected at the Kennington Rd end. The down track across Deptford Bridge, and part of the down over Westminster Bridge, have been relaid. (Details of Stage II replacement buses omitted).

5.3.51
Recently repainted cars include:- 105, 334, 337, 1628, 1828, 1829, 1906, 1935. New turnouts have been inserted in Plumstead High St. The down between Gresham Rd. Brixton and the railway bridges has been relaid. The inside curve at Westminster has been renewed. Work has been going on for some time on the conversion of Abbey Wood depot. work has; also started on Camberwell and New Cross depots, necessitating the use by some New Cross cars of Penhall Rd as a running depot.

19.4.51
(Details of Stage III replacement buses omitted). The Charing Cross and Savoy St crossovers have been relaid, also the trailing points of the disused or little-used connection at Goose Green. Relaying has also taken place on the up just east of Rye Lane. The following cars have been repainted- 105, 133, 159, 380, 395, 1779, 1812, 1Bl9, 1844, 1845, 1854, 1862, 1867, 1955, 1965.

18.6.51
The following track renewals have been made recently: down south of Agricultural Hall junc.; northern half of down track on Bostall Hill; facing exit points from Marshalsea Rd. at Boro' Stn.; facing exit points from London Rd. at St. George's Circus - part only); part of both tracks east of Wickham La.; Middle Park Ave. (south side of roundabout); crossover at Forest Hill Stn. (part only); parts of both downhill roads on Dog Kennel Hill, and parts of both tracks at the top of the Hill. These cars have been repainted:- 101, 111, 120, 203, 210, 297, 342, 1804, 1811, 1854, 1887, 1934.

76

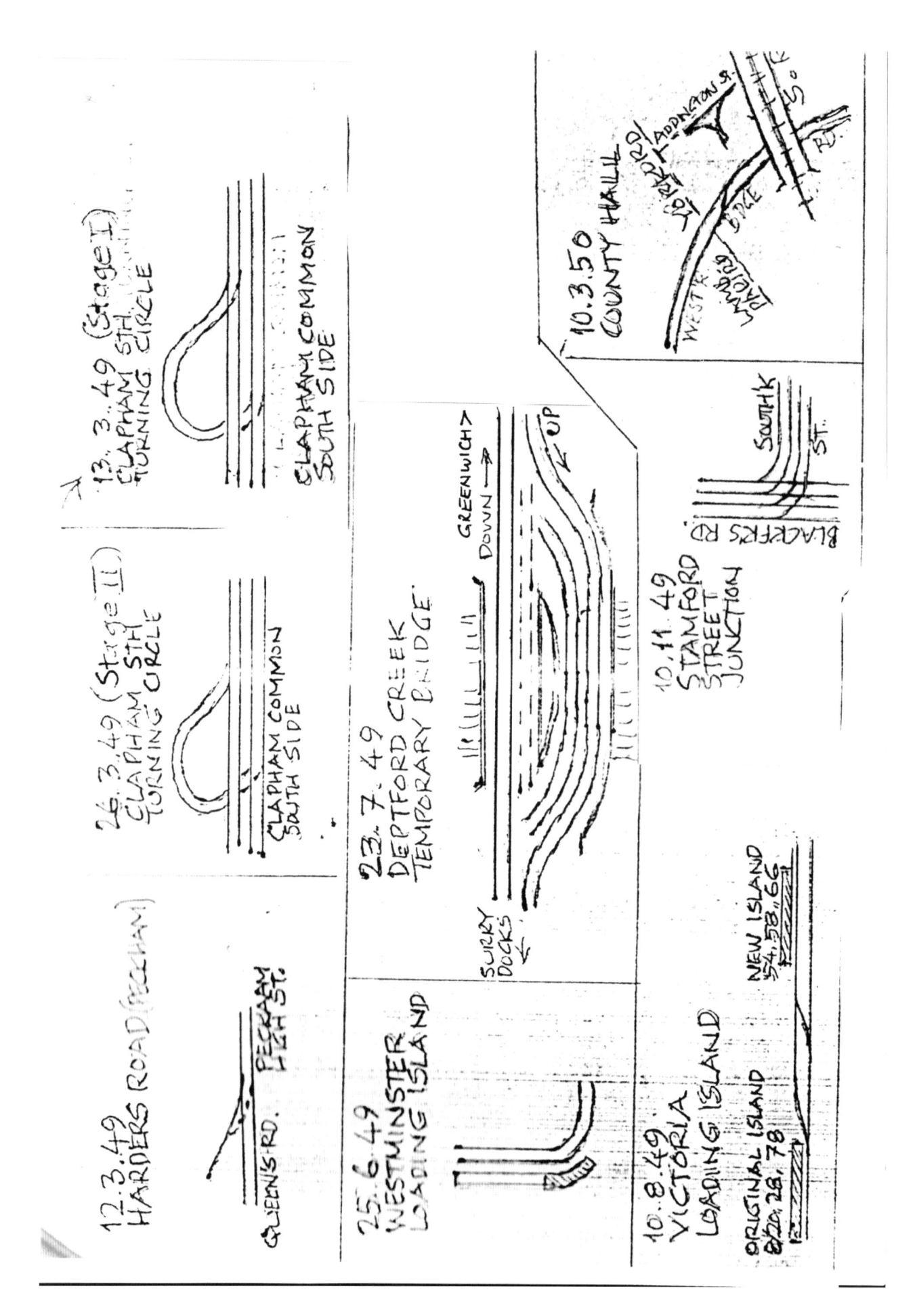

77

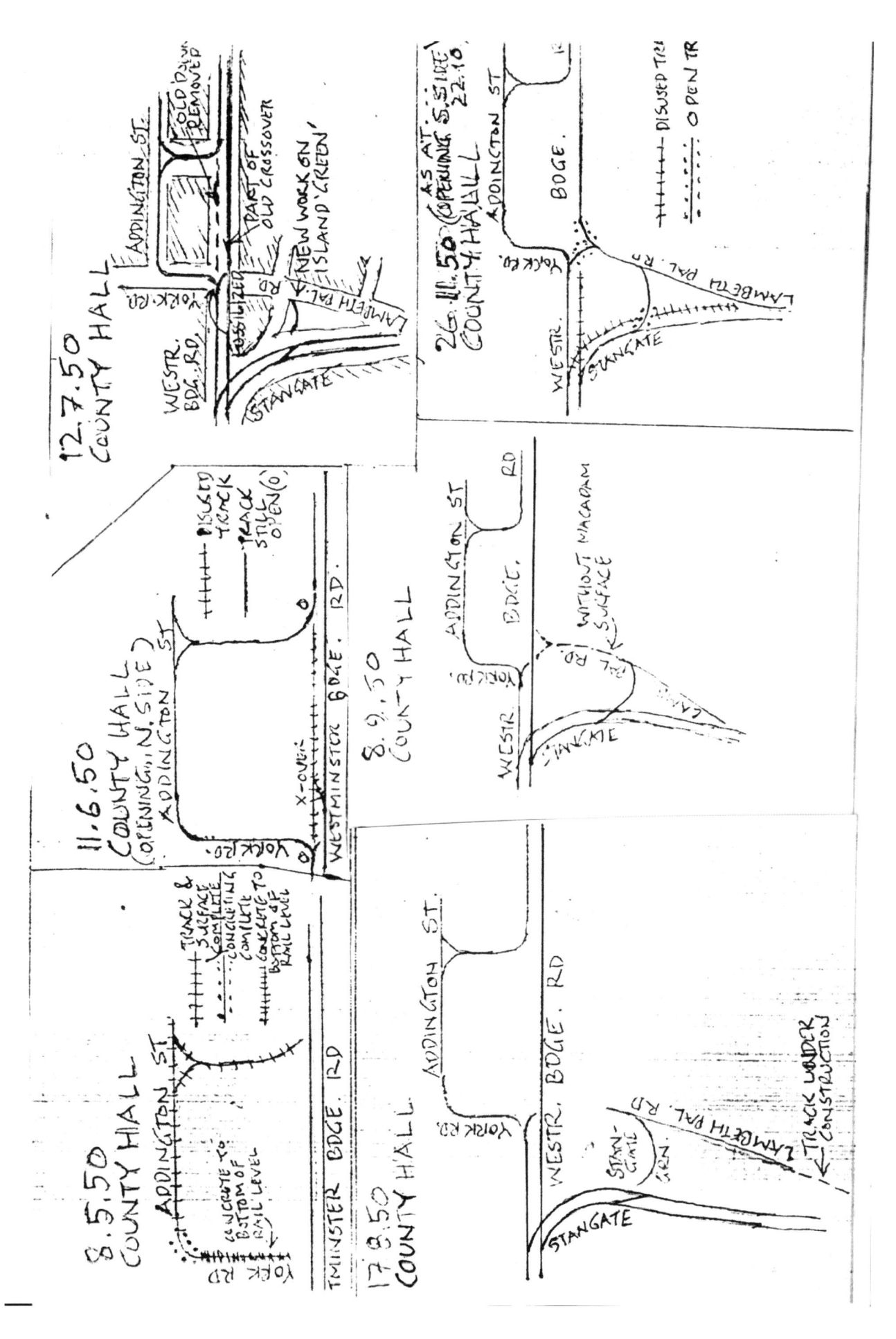

Appendix B

The following extract is from the magazine *JOHN BULL*, 23 September 1950.

During the night of September 30 a long and melancholy procession will trundle across South London from Clapham to Charlton. Clanging, swaying, occasionally wheezing a little, the trams from routes numbers 12, 26, 28, 31 and 34 will be making their last journey. Within a couple of years, most of the 800 London tramcars will have followed their leaders into the "tramatorium"; their lines will have been taken up behind them. London's trams will be no more. Some of the retired cars will be sold to outside purchasers - Leeds is taking ninety-six of the more "modern" (only eighteen years old) for £500 each - and, a few may finish up on allotments and as stationary caravans. Car Number 1 will go into London Transport's Museum. But most will be stripped, broken up and burnt. A thousand buses will replace them. Whatever advantages there may be in the change - and London Transport is satisfied there is an overwhelming case for it - only the most unsentimental person, watching that stately procession, will not have a lump in his throat.

The men who have worked on trams all their lives will be among the sorriest - and happiest - to see them go. "It's forty-two years since I first called out 'Fares, please,'" says a plump, double-chinned conductor, "Monty" Wood. "I tell you, it's hard and responsible work shepherding passengers on and off at every stop. I'll be glad when we transfer to the buses and can go safely up to the kerb to pick people up and put them off. Still, I expect I'll miss the old rattler - a tram seems to have a personality all its own. I've learnt a lot about human nature on this job. We can spot those passengers who are going to try to diddle the conductor almost at a glance."

Before the war the most popular tram passenger was the wine and spirits traveller who regularly gave away quarter-bottles of whisky and gin; not so popular was the South London butcher who caught several conductors by offering them a leg of lamb on the top deck for a shilling, saying he would leave it downstairs for them: when they opened it they found it was just a bundle of fats. And there is always the drunk whose friends subscribe a shilling for the conductor to put him off at a street corner

"Sometimes they don't go so easily," says Monty. "Once I had a really tough navvy upstairs. I tried to get him off the car, but he hooked his feet round the rail and I couldn't move him. My driver stopped the tram and came round to help me. Just then I saw Bombardier Billy Wells, the boxing champion, walking along the street. 'Give us a hand, Billy,' I called out, and he came and unhooked the bloke's legs. Just recently I had a drunk who was a bit more peaceful. I stuck him up against a lamp-post and said, 'You wait here for me.' When we came by two hours later, he was still there.''

Monty Wood's regular driver, chirpy, bushy-eyebrowed George Clifford ("Cliff"), is even more pleased than Monty at the switch to buses. "I'll be able to sit down at last!" he says, sighing in anticipation of comfort. Like every other tram-driver who so wishes, he has undergone a fortnight's intensive instruction at Chiswick Training School on the mechanics and driving of oil buses. For the first time Cliff has learnt to drive a vehicle which is not fixed in its course. "How to steer was the hardest thing to learn, and the feeling that I could dodge about a bit in the roadway was very strange at first, he says. His wife Bet is also pleased at his new job.

Before he became a tram-driver, fifty-year-old Cliff worked on the permanent way, laying and repairing tracks. "When I came out of the Army after the first World War tram-driving was a coveted job, and I had to wait ten years before they could take me," he explains. In that time he had daily tussles with live wires. "Once a cat got down the centre conduit and, wearing a rubber glove, I had to put my hand down and feel along the live 600-volt rail for it. I had almost grabbed it when it jumped on my arm. If it had landed, and touched me and the rail at the same time, I should have been a goner, so I drew back quickly. Then I managed to get hold of its tail, swing it up and throw it on the road. It got up and walked into Greenwich Church as if it was drunk."

Trams have to obey the 30-m.p.h. speed limit like any other vehicle, and drivers have been fined for speeding. One driver used to put his head out of his cab and warn motorists that they were coming into a speed trap - until one day he told a military-looking man to look out, and found he was speaking to a Scotland Yard official. When the trams now scheduled for the scrapheap came into service in 1905, a driver was fined £1 for exceeding 10 m.p.h. in Greenwich Road.

It was the police and Parliament who objected when a young American, George Francis Train, introduced tramways into England in 1860. They argued that the rails, which stuck up half an inch, were dangerous. The tramway had to be removed. However, progress and the fact that rails gave a much smoother ride than the bumpy roads of those days - could not be denied, and, after the passing of the Tramways Act, 1870, horses pulling carriages along lines were to be seen all over London and the provinces. Carters discovered that the lines made their horses' job easier, too, and showed no compunction about slowing down the trams while they leisurely proceeded along the tracks. When a West Ham carter left his horse-van unattended for fifty minutes, thus disorganizing the tram service, the bench refused to convict him of obstruction on the ground that the tramway department should have diverted the trams.

E/3 class car 1992 is depicted on the last day of service 33, as it works under overhead wires on the West Norwood section. Someone at London Transport has chalked FOR EXPORT on the fender indicating that electrical and mechanical equipment from this vehicle had just been purchased by Alexandria. After a delay the Egyptian city recycled its purchases in 1955.

Appendix C
London Trams in Colour

Gresham Road, Brixton was the site of the switch from conduit to overhead trolley on service 34. The 34 was the only post war route to pass two such changeover points on its circuitous journey from Chelsea, Kings Road to Blackfriars, John Carpenter Street; the other was at the Camberwell end of Coldharbour Lane. The full trip was timed at just under the hour; the service interval of 5 to 6 minutes between cars as far as Camberwell Green was more frequent than the section from there to the Embankment. Note the two change pit attendants and the fork for inserting ploughs into the carrier under each tramcar. Car 1395 had a long life which ended in October 1950, a couple of weeks after the 34 succumbed to bus route 45. *C.Carter*

Ex
THOUSANDS ARE FINDING STRENGTH IN GUINNESS
133
POST IT TO

40
SAVOY ST STRAND
LAST TRAM WEEK
ON JULY 5 WE SAY GOODBYE TO LONDON
1939
LAST TRAM WEEK

Plenty of activity is depicted here at the junction of Brixton Road, Effra Road and Acre Lane, as UCC Feltham car 2129 waits for the lights to change before resuming its journey towards central London. Allocated to Telford Avenue Depot, it has been inserted as an extra into the service. This vehicle was subsequently sold to Leeds, where it received the fleet number 574. *C.Carter*

Trams are attracting more than the usual attention on the final day of operation in London. Intending passengers attempt to board car 1939 in New Cross Road outside New Cross Depot. As was usual in the capital, granite setts border both tram tracks. They formed a durable road surface, but became very slippery when wet. *C.Carter*

Another last day scene on the Victoria Embankment features car 1950 as it loads passengers. Chalked inscriptions on the tram lament the passing of an old friend. Come nightfall this stretch of track will be thronged by sightseers and well wishers. Many of whom placed pennies on the rails to be crushed by the final tramcars. *F.Ward*

E/1 class car 1406 heads towards New Cross Gate; it is probably on a depot working. Note the distinctive BISTO advertisement, which adorned many of London's trams in the post war period. Service 66 ran between Forest Hill and Victoria, it ceased on 6th October 1951. Car 1406 was scrapped at Penhall Road in January 1952. *C.Carter*

Car 85 formed part of a contribution made to the LPTB by East Ham Corporation in 1933. Originally these vehicles stayed on their home patch in East London, but were later transferred to Abbey Wood Depot, after they fell victim to the trolleybus conversion programme. Here in Woolwich High Street there was time for the conductor to raise the trolley before reaching the change pit on Market Hill. The other four overhead wires supplied power for the 696/698 trolleybuses a few yards in advance of their terminus at Parsons Hill. *C.Carter*

Views of Penhall Road scrap yard evoke strong feelings among tramway enthusiasts. Two Feltham type tramcars have been stored prior to their removal north to Leeds, where they will see out service until the West Yorkshire system closed late in 1959. In this respect they were more fortunate than the hundreds of 'standards' that were burnt on the spot. *C. Carter*

Framed by one of the arches of Waterloo Bridge, car 1858 makes its last journeys along the Embankment on 5th July 1952. The previous day it had been purchased by Peter Davis, therefore legally it was now on hire to London Transport. Later that day in the quieter roads of Eltham Peter did get a turn 'on the handles', driving his tramcar. Logically he should have asked for a share of the day's takings as rent! Car 1858 now gives rides to visitors at a transport museum in Carlton Colville near Lowestoft. *C. Carter*

In Blackfriars Road car 578 is about to cross the junction with Southwark Street. Note the dent in the dash and the missing service number stencil. Advertising hoardings brightened up the post war streets of South London. Often they were positioned by vacant plots caused by the Blitz. In the UK Biro pens, named after their inventor, were first licensed in 1938.
C.Carter

The Temple Underground Station on the District and Circle lines offers passengers a quicker way of navigating the capital than either the bus or the tram. The latter is on the long run to Abbey Wood, right on the border of the County of London. The bus on route 109 replaced the 16/18 trams on 7th April 1951. Mixed traffic of diesel buses and tramcars along what was originally a tram only right of way raised a few eyebrows among LTE officials. It occasioned several accidents and near misses. *C.Carter*

Woolwich Road, Charlton first saw horse trams in passenger service on Saturday, 4th June 1881. Car 1926 is a few hours away from bringing down the tramway curtain at this location. As was usual in Great Britain, the tram tracks have been paved with granite setts, whilst the rest of the road was surfaced in asphalt. A solitary dustbin stands next to the 'request' tram stop. Perhaps it was thoughtfully provided for used tickets? *F. Ward*

Abbey Wood Depot always had a reputation for keeping its vehicles in 'good nick', as demonstrated here with car 299 at Eltham Green. This particular tram had started life as a member of the West Ham Corporation Tramways fleet. It was always identifiable by the single pane of glass in the top deck window just above the 44 indicator. Because of the position of their advertisement mouldings these class WH cars did not carry the LAST TRAM WEEK posters. *C. Carter*

Woolwich change pit on Market Hill was a favourite spot for photographers. Here Clarence Carter has managed to capture a tram, a trolleybus and in the distance a bus at the terminus of route 75. Trolleybus route 698 replaced the Erith trams in 1935 and was extended to Woolwich from Abbey Wood, thereby working in tandem with trams on services 36/38/40. Car 1957 has a leaking driver's vestibule; a couple of small sandbags offer a temporary solution to the ingress of rain water!
C.Carter

The Little Market by the tram stop in Woolwich was a survivor of a whole row of small shops wiped out in the Blitz on the approach road to Woolwich Free Ferry. The conductor of E/1 class car 1565 grapples with the trolley rope to hoist the pole. Note the adverts for Swan Vestas - the Smokers' Match, Andrews Liver Salts and Puritan Soap. It has to be remembered wartime rationing affecting goods and foodstuffs lingered on in the UK until 1954. *C.Carter*

54
VICTORIA
...and Hovis and butter for tea
560
CHEMIST
SAYERS & BARNES
ORANGE

46
LAST TRAM WEEK
ON JULY 5 WE SAY GOODBYE TO LONDON
LONDON TRANSPORT
187

Catford was once well served by electric traction. The leading car 560 on service 54 has been curtailed in its journey to Grove Park and is about to reverse in order to return to Victoria. Folk desirous of going all the way to Downham and beyond have been transferred to the following vehicle. Supervised by an inspector, who is just crossing the road, trams could be very flexible in responding to passenger flows. *C.Carter*

This E/3 class car 187 was originally the property of Leyton Council, but included in the LCC fleet and first stationed at Bow Depot. Here on Southwark Bridge it awaits the influx of last day crowds before departing on its hour long journey to Woolwich via Eltham. Two weeks after this photo was taken it was scrapped at Penhall Road. *C.Carter*

The powerful four motor HR/2 class vehicles worked the Dog Kennel Hill services. Car 1876 approaches Forest Hill, as it heads for Blackwall Tunnel by way of Catford, Lewisham and Greenwich. Supplying a necessary link across South London, tram service 58 was replaced by bus route 185 on 6th October 1951. *C.Carter*

Car 1917 mingles with the traffic at Kennington. On the far left of the picture next to the Austin van we glimpse a standard 1950s LCC ambulance. Once a hub of tramway activity, by the time of this view only tram services 40 and 72 survived. The Horns Tavern on the right laid claim to be the founding home of Surrey Cricket Club; it was severely damaged by a 'doodlebug' V1 flying bomb in August 1944. *C.Carter*

A tower wagon has been summoned to sort out a problem with the overhead wires at the Yorkshire Grey roundabout, Eltham Green. Meanwhile cars 560 and 1909 creep gingerly past. The latter has been curtailed at Eltham Church and through passengers to Beresford Square will have to change on to car 560. Prominent in this picture are a number of traction standards. After abandonment a batch of these poles was sold to Portsmouth for a new trolleybus extension in that city. *C.Carter*

The frequency and reliability of trams on services 44, 46 and 72 left an indelible mark on the locals. Somehow the replacing buses never managed to live up to their railbound predecessors. Cheap fares also helped to fill seats here at Eltham Green, as people pile on car 1855. By taking the bypass route along Westhorne Avenue these folk are probably on their way to shopping in Woolwich. *C.Carter*

London Transport staff line the approach to New Cross Depot. Around noon on the last day car 1966 waits to take up service. One can only guess what the drivers, conductors and repair staff felt about the loss of their trams. Sadly the building, one of the largest of its type in the UK, had gained a reputation for lax maintenance standards, in contrast to other establishments on the system. Disruption occasioned by the conversion to a bus garage, which had commenced some months before the last tram quit the place, had not helped the matter. In fact planning setbacks delayed completion until the spring of 1954. *C.Carter*

In one of the classic images of the tramway era a modern Feltham type shares the tracks with two 'standards'. One of the reasons the LCC adopted the costly conduit was to avoid the perceived intrusive presence of overhead wires at sensitive locations such as we see here. The same aesthetic argument for an open skyline also hampered the development of trolleybuses in London. *W. Robertson*

The centre of Greenwich has avoided the civic vandalism inflicted on its Woolwich neighbour, consequently this scene in Nelson Road has changed very little since horse tram days. Car 87 with a full load on the lower deck clatters over the triangular junction as it heads east towards Abbey Wood. *C. Carter*

As at 1st January 1950 car 1363 was included in the inventory of Abbey Wood Depot. Here it stands on the single track in Abbey Wood Road; the depot building is on the left of the picture. Although constructed in the first decade of the twentieth century, the tram still looks good for a few years further work. Unfortunately its fate had already been decided and it was scrapped in March 1951. The depot itself was rebuilt for buses and later closed in October 1981. It has since been demolished. *W. Robertson*

Two trams are depicted in McLeod Road just yards from the county border with Kent. The rails will shortly veer to their left in order to reach the terminus in Knee Hill outside the Harrow Inn. Note the six wire overhead which also accommodated trolleybuses on route 698. At this time Abbey Wood was served exclusively by electric traction. *C. Carter*

Bibliography

An extensive bibliography is to be found in *Lord Ashfield's Trams* (ISBN 978-1-85414-384-6). An addition to the list is the excellent *London's Last Trams* (ISBN 978-1-874422-94-4) by Hugh Taylor. Another addition is a work of fiction, *Camberwell Beauties* (ISBN 0-552-11039-6) by Ralph Harris, published by Corgi in 1979. Originally described as - an earthy story about a tram driver, his colourful friends and amorous adventures - it is rather tame by 2023 standards, but contains many detailed descriptions of London and its trams.

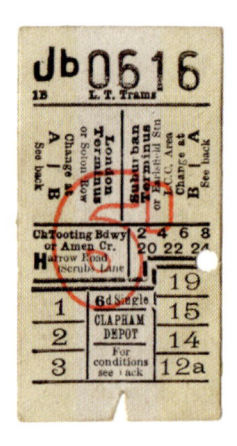

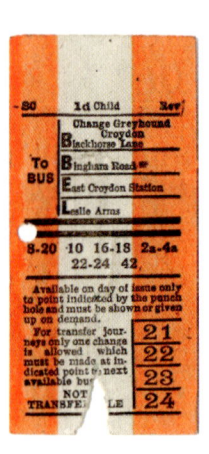

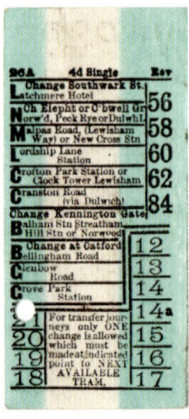

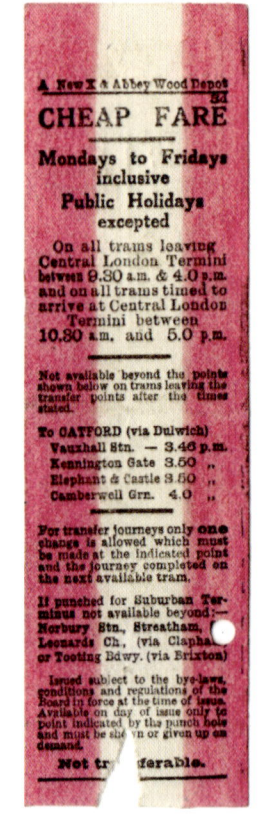

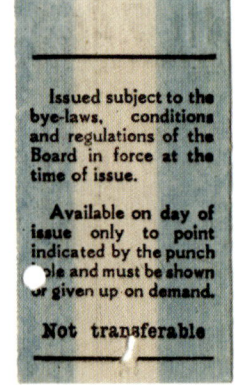